HEALTHY BODIES, HEALTHY MINDS

by Denise Bieniek, M.S.
Illustrated by Dan Regan

Troll
CREATIVE
TEACHER
IDEAS

Troll Creative Teacher Ideas was designed to help today's dedicated, time-pressured teacher. Created by teachers for teachers, this innovative series provides a wealth of classroom ideas to help reinforce important concepts and stimulate your students' creative thinking skills.

Each book in the series focuses on a different curriculum theme to give you the flexibility to teach any given skill at any time of the year. The wide range of ideas and activities included in each book are certain to help you create an atmosphere where students are continually eager to learn new concepts and develop important skills.

We hope this comprehensive series will provide you with everything you need to foster a fun and challenging learning environment for your students. **Troll Creative Teacher Ideas** is a resource you'll turn to again and again!

Titles in this series:

Classroom Decor:
Decorate Your Classroom from Bulletin Boards to Time Lines

Creative Projects: Quick and Easy Art Projects

Earth Alert: Environmental Studies for Grades 4-6

Explore the World: Social Studies Projects and Activities

Healthy Bodies, Healthy Minds

Holidays Around the World: Multicultural Projects and Activities

It All Adds Up: Math Skill-Building Activities for Grades 4-6

Learning Through Literature:
Projects and Activities for Linking Literature and Writing

Story Writing: Creative Writing Projects and Activities

Think About It: Skill-Building Puzzles Across the Curriculum

The World Around Us: Geography Projects and Activities

World Explorers: Discover the Past

Metric Conversion Chart

1 inch = 2.54 cm	1 foot = .305 m	1 yard = .914 m
1 mile = 1.61 km	1 fluid ounce = 29.573 ml	1 cup = .24 l
1 pint = .473 l	1 teaspoon = 4.93 ml	1 tablespoon = 14.78 ml

Contents

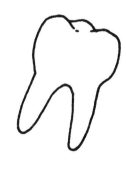

Five Senses Vocabulary

5 senses Dictionary

Name _____

Read the words below. Then write each one under the appropriate heading(s).

lens	nasal passage	auditory canal	olfactory bulb
sclera	odors	iris	Pacinian corpuscles
hammer	trigeminal system	eardrum	epiglottis
cornea	taste buds	Merkel's disks	pupil
auricle	olfactory cortex	stirrup	optic nerve
retina	Eustachian tube	epidermis	cochlea

Vision   Smell   Taste

_____   _____   _____
_____   _____   _____
_____   _____   _____
_____   _____   _____
_____   _____   _____
_____   _____   _____
_____

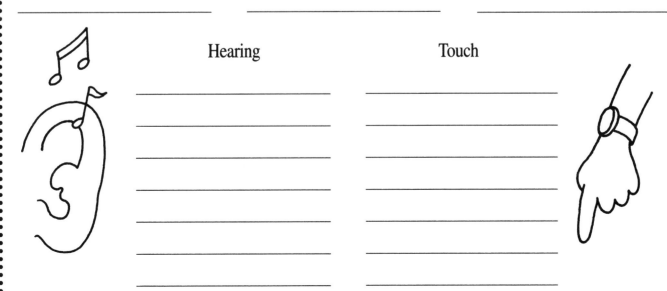

Hearing   Touch

_____   _____
_____   _____
_____   _____
_____   _____
_____   _____
_____   _____

Cause and Effect

cause ↓
Achooooo...
Effect ↗

Name _____

Read each group of sentences. Then decide which sentence caused the action, which sentence tells about the effect the action had, and which sentence is unrelated to the action. Write "Cause" next to the cause, "Effect" next to the effect, and "Other" next to the unrelated sentence.

1. _____ Dad was baking apple-cinnamon muffins.
   _____ The smell of muffins was all over the house.
   _____ I like blueberry muffins.

2. _____ She added more sugar to the lemonade.
   _____ Soda contains a lot of sugar.
   _____ When I took a sip of the lemonade, my lips puckered.

3. _____ The pizza had pepperoni and peppers on it.
   _____ My tongue was burned on the first bite.
   _____ The pizza was served hot from the oven.

4. _____ I couldn't hear the next morning.
   _____ We sat by the speakers at the concert.
   _____ I got a great T-shirt at the concert.

5. _____ The light was very bright.
   _____ 100-watt bulbs are expensive.
   _____ His pupils dilated.

6. _____ The garden was filled with fragrant flowers.
   _____ Her nose was all stuffed up from her cold.
   _____ The breeze carried the odor to the neighbor's yard.

7. _____ He prefers sweet food.
   _____ She prefers salty food.
   _____ She bought pretzels and potato chips at the store.

Mixed-Up Sentences

Head my my is brain in!

False

Name _____

Unscramble the word order of each sentence and rewrite it correctly on the line provided. Decide if the sentence is true or false. Then write *T* or *F* in the space next to each scrambled sentence.

1. Body cells carry to red parts your of blood oxygen all. ____

    _____

2. Hemisphere the controls the left cerebral side body the of left. ____

    _____

3. System together brain and form cord spinal nervous the central the. ____

    _____

4. Retina control the enlarges and amount of contracts to light the through passing the pupil. ____

    _____

5. Are located taste buds in papillae the on tongue fungiform the. ____

    _____

6. Strike the sound and cause vibrate waves cochlea it to. ____

    _____

7. Air goes into inhaled esophagus and the bronchi two the. ____

    _____

8. Used speaking for laughing and the larynx singing is. ____

    _____

9. Digestive is produced juice bile a by glands the salivary. ____

    _____

10. Skeletal three muscle: there types are smooth cardiac and of. ____

    _____

Healthy Syllables

skel-e-ton

Name _____

Figure out the number of syllables in each word in the list below. Then write each word under column head with the matching number of syllables. If you need help, use a dictionary.

axon	cerebrum	cilia	dendrites
epiglottis	lens	melanin	mucus
neuron	pupil	synapse	cell
venae cavae	fetus	skeleton	chromosomes
genes	brain	nerves	reflex
memory	muscle	emotions	dreams
lungs	diaphragm	alveoli	pancreas
esophagus	incisors	stomach	aorta

1   **2**   **3**   **4**

Body Labels

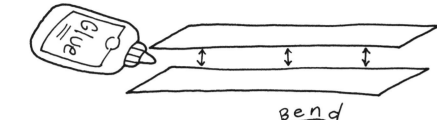

MATERIALS:

crayons or markers
scissors
oaktag
glue
3" x 5" index cards
tape

DIRECTIONS:

1. Reproduce the art on pages 10–13. Color the body shapes, mount them on oaktag, and cut them out.

2. Glue two 2" x 6" strips of oaktag together. Bend the strips in half to make a stand for each body cutout.

3. Glue the stand in place on each body cutout.

4. Cut 3" x 5" index cards in half widthwise to make name labels for each body system: nervous system, digestive system, respiratory system, and circulatory system. Tape each sign card to the bottom of the appropriate body cutout.

5. Next, cut more index cards into 1" x 3" pieces. Then cut one of the short ends on each piece so it resembles the point of an arrow.

6. Write the names of the major parts of each system on these labels. Then tape them onto the appropriate spots on the body cutouts, as shown, making sure the point of each card is placed correctly.

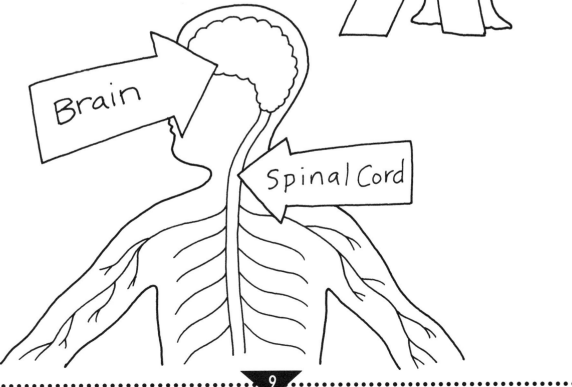

9

Body Labels

Body Labels

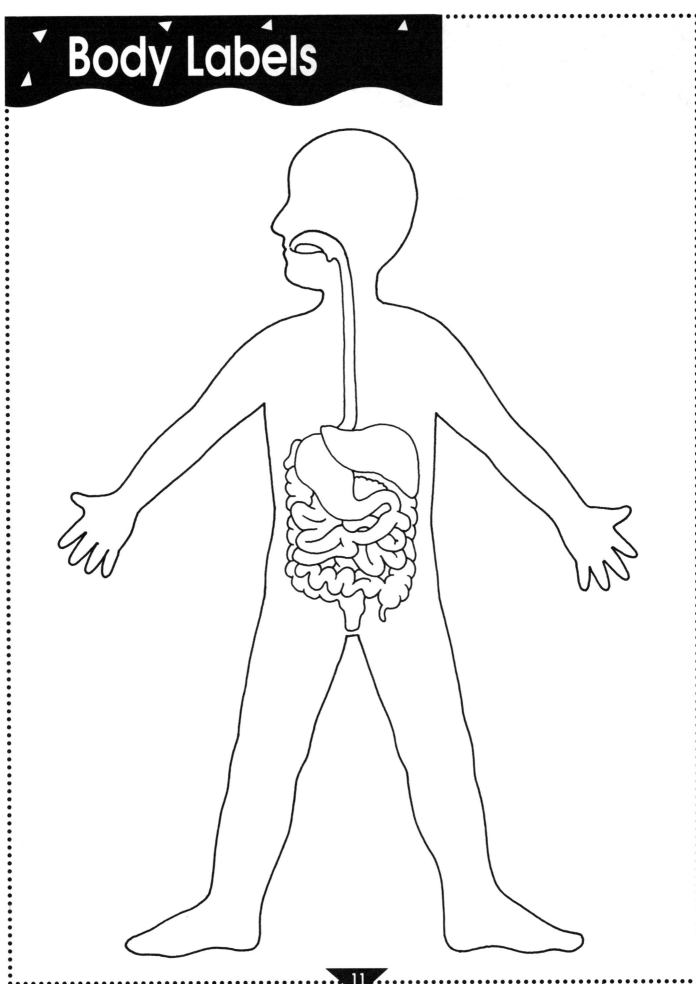

Body Labels

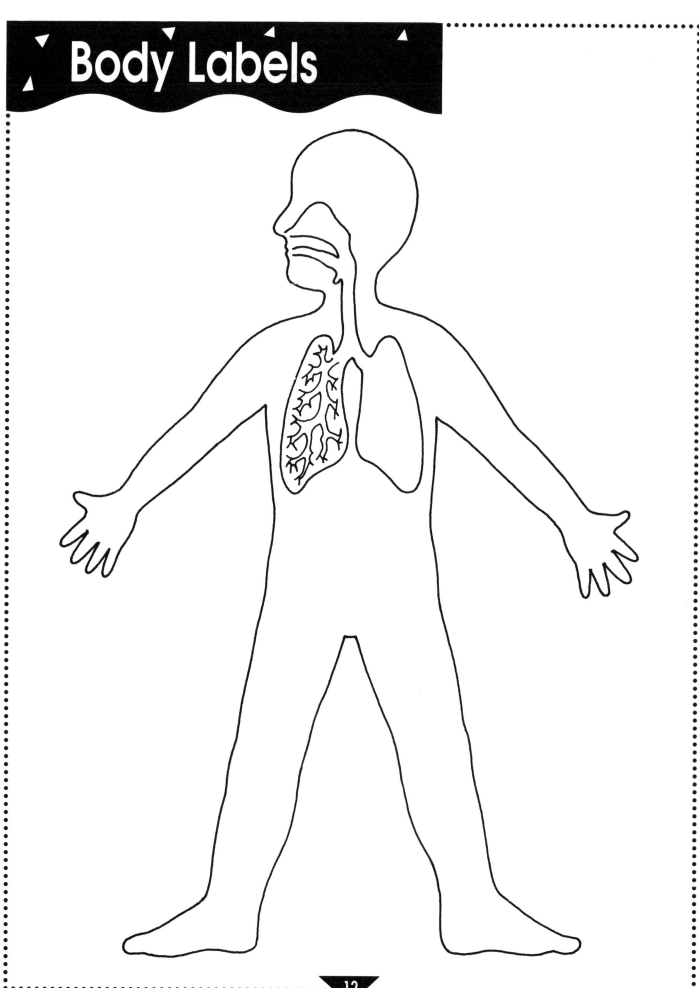

Body Labels

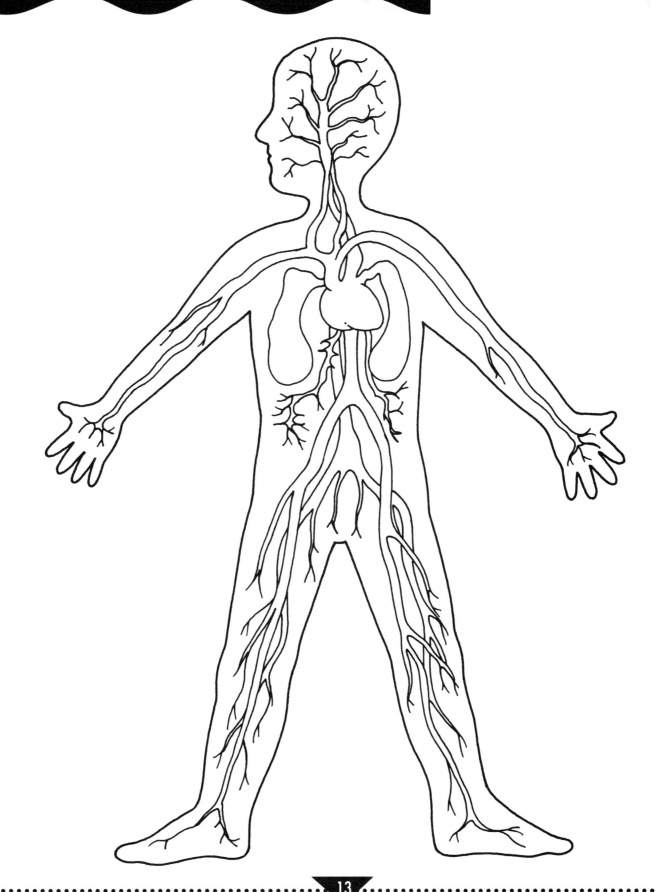

Felt Body Puzzle

MATERIALS:

crayons or markers
scissors
felt scraps
glue
2' x 5' piece of felt

DIRECTIONS:

1. Reproduce the art on pages 15–19. Color the body part shapes and cut them out.
2. Glue scraps of felt to the back of each major organ.
3. Have a volunteer lay on a 2' x 5' piece of felt. Trace his or her outline onto the felt. (Make sure his or her face is in profile.) Cut out the body shape. (If the volunteer's body is too long, have him or her bend at the knees to try to fit.)
4. Ask volunteers to identify and describe each organ.
5. Attach the felt body shape to the wall. Distribute one organ each to a small group of students. Ask each student to place the organ he or she is holding onto the appropriate place on the felt body.
6. Leave the organs near the felt body so students may use the activity during their free time.

Felt Body Puzzle

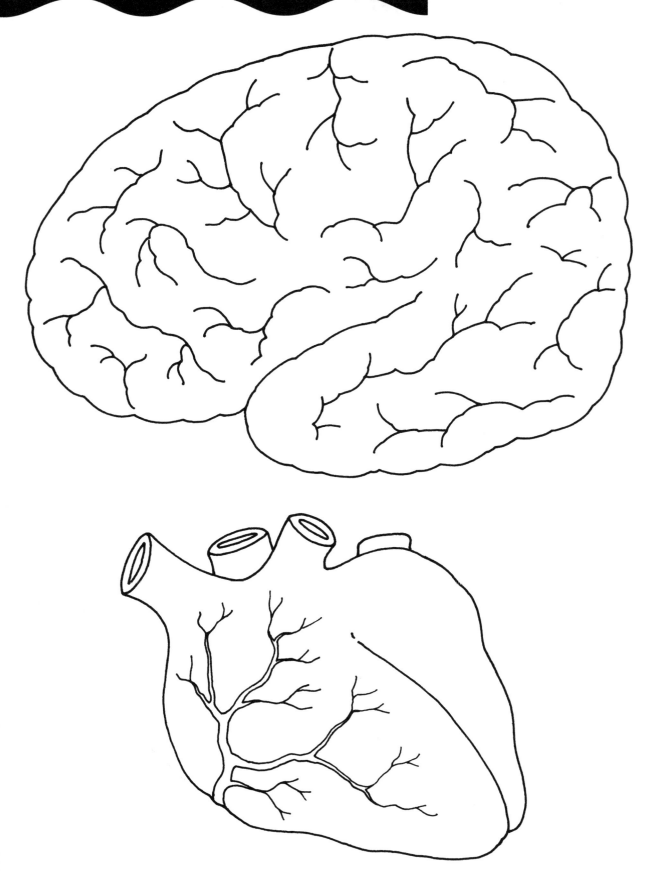

Felt Body Puzzle

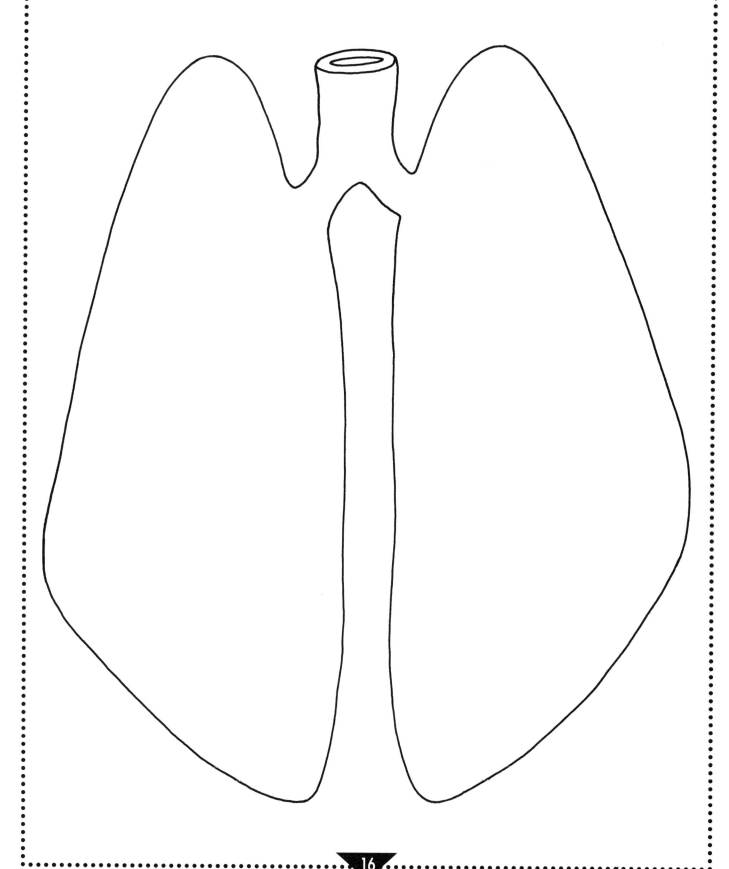

Felt Body Puzzle

Felt Body Puzzle

Felt Body Puzzle

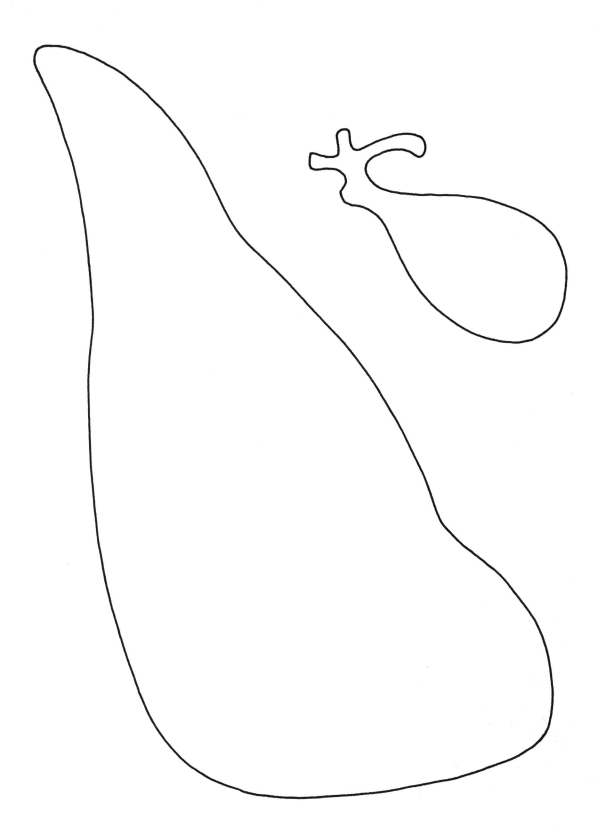

An Inside View

I vant your 15 across!

Name _____

Identify the word that each clue is describing and write it in the appropriate box.

Across

1. Body parts specialized for the perception of sound.
3. Bony framework of a human being.
6. Organs that can be contracted and expanded to produce bodily movements.
8. Organ that receives blood from the veins and pumps it through the arteries.
10. The lower parts of the alimentary canal.
13. The outermost layer of the skin, having no blood vessels and consisting of several layers of cells, covering the dermis.
14. Organs capable of inflation to receive and contain liquids or gases.
15. The fluid that circulates in the heart, arteries, and veins.
16. The organs of sight.

Down

2. Saclike organ into which food passes from the esophagus.
4. Secretes bile and plays an important role in metabolism.
5. Two respiratory organs that oxygenate and remove carbon dioxide from blood.
7. Main part of the nervous system; located in the cranium.
9. Sight, smell, taste, hearing, and touch. (Two words.)
11. Used for biting, tearing, and chewing.
12. Thick bundle of nerve tissue of the central nervous system. (Two words.)

Bone Word Search

Better "bone" up on your anatomy!

Name _____

In the puzzle below, find the names of the bones listed in the box. Circle the words when you have found them. Words may be written forward, backward, up, down, or diagonally.

```
R F E C L A V I C H O M R D T S C
I P U M E T A P H L O A R A D I O
C O A X L S I S Y G F T I B O I A
O R O R B S U Z Y E I I B U I L X
S C R I I I D I O L P R P Z Y G O
C S R Y D E H Y O C A L U P A C S
O L U A N H T A M I T E M M P T O
P A R L A L Y A B V E A R I E T E
A S C L M L G I L A T N O R F F A
I R A E V Y T O A L L L N A M D X
T A P T Z D S I R C L U F E M U O
E T R A A I G D O H M R P H A L C
T A L P N O R F P H A L A N G E S
L T S S Z Y G O M A T I C Y H D O
L E O Y Y H U M E R U S U L T R A
A M A L U B I F T A L C V I C L E
```

parietal	frontal	temporal	zygomatic
mandible	hyoid	sternum	clavicle
scapula	humerus	ulna	radius
phalanges	ribs	femur	patella
tibia	fibula	metatarsal	os coxae

© 1996 Troll Creative Teacher Ideas

Chicken Lessons

Purchase and cook a whole chicken for a meal at home. After the meat has been eaten, save the bones.

Put the bones in a large pot of boiling water. As the remainder of material on the bones softens, scrape it off with a fork or knife.

When the chicken's skeleton is bare, take apart the larger bones and leave the smaller bones together. Place all the bones in a resealable plastic bag.

Have children reassemble the skeleton on a large piece of oaktag. Allow time for students to handle the chicken bones gently. Ask volunteers to compare and contrast them to human bones. When all the bones have been used, a whole chicken skeleton should be laid out on the oaktag.

Store the bones in the plastic bag with the oaktag drawing.

"Believe It Or Not!" Bulletin Board

Largest Human Waist: 119 inches

Longest Hiccup Spell: 69 years 5 months

"Believe It Or N

MATERIALS:

bright bulletin board paper
stapler
9" x 12" construction paper
crayons or markers

DIRECTIONS:

1. Staple bright paper to a bulletin board. Inform the class that they will be creating a "Believe It Or Not!" bulletin board. The board will display facts about extraordinary body features. Brainstorm with the class some topics about the body in which viewers of the board might be interested, such as the brain, or the smallest person in the world.

2. Bring the class to the library to research their topics. One good source is the *Guinness Book of World Records*. Some suggestions for the bulletin board:

• The largest adult waist so far recorded is 119 inches.

• The smallest adult waist so far recorded is 13 inches.

• The cells in the human body with the longest life are the brain cells, which last for life.

• The most common contagious disease in the world is the common cold.

• The record for the longest spell of hiccups is 69 years, 5 months.

3. Each student in the class may choose one fact to illustrate, then write the fact on the bottom of the paper. Distribute construction paper and crayons or markers to the class. Ask them to imagine what each fact might look like and what life might be like for the person who set the record (if applicable). After drawing their interpretations of their chosen facts, students may wish to add their imagined insights to their papers.

4. Staple the work to the bulletin board. Then title the board "Believe It Or Not!"

23

Oatcakes and Fruit

Students will love making and eating this nutritious snack.

MATERIALS:

2 cups flour
2 cups quick-cooking oats
4 tablespoons sugar
4 teaspoons baking powder
2 teaspoons baking soda
1 teaspoon salt (optional)
3 cups buttermilk
1 cup nonfat milk
4 tablespoons vegetable oil
4 eggs
strawberries, peaches, blueberries, or other fruit

DIRECTIONS:

1. Combine all ingredients into a large mixing bowl and beat with a wire whisk or electric mixer until smooth.
2. Heat an electric skillet and spray it with non-stick cooking spray.
3. Pour about 1/8-cup batter onto the hot skillet for each oatcake. When the top of the oatcake bubbles, turn it over and cook the other side.
4. Sprinkle fruit on top of hot oatcakes and serve.
YIELD: Approximately 40-48 oatcakes

Name _____

Fill in the lines at the end of each statement with an explanation of why the sentence is true. Then share your answers with the class.

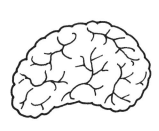 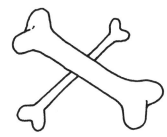 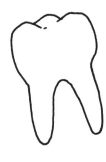 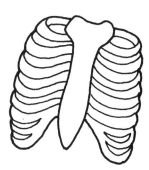

1. The brain is the most complex organ in the body because _____

_____

2. Ribs are shaped the way they are because _____

_____

3. Bones and muscles work together because _____

_____

4. Teeth must be strong because _____

_____

5. New blood is being produced constantly because _____

_____

6. People's hair, eye, and skin colors tend to resemble those of their parents because _____

_____

7. Organs are shaped the way they are because _____

_____

8. The nerves deliver messages all over the body because _____

_____

Relevant or Irrelevant?

Name _____

Cross out the word in each group that is not relevant to the first word listed on the left.

1. brain	cerebellum	cerebrum	anvil
2. heart	atrium	retina	aorta
3. lungs	diaphragm	trachea	dermis
4. spinal cord	pelvis	dendrites	reflex
5. eye	iris	pancreas	cornea
6. digestion	bile	hormones	saliva
7. blood	tibia	plasma	veins
8. genes	hair	height	femur
9. epidermis	sebaceous glands	marrow	melanin
10. skeleton	hypothermia	mandible	joint
11. exercise	pulse	muscles	larynx
12. healing	leukocyte	clotting	palate

Body Tours

Name _____

Pretend that you are a travel agent trying to sell tours inside the human body. Write a sentence or two about each attraction tourists would enjoy seeing. Make your pitch as exciting and interesting as possible!

1. BRAIN

2. MOUTH

3. HEART

4. LUNGS

5. STOMACH

6. SPINAL CORD

7. FINGERS

8. KNEE

1. _____
_____
_____

2. _____
_____

3. _____
_____
_____

4. _____
_____
_____

5. _____
_____

6. _____
_____

7. _____
_____
_____

8. _____
_____

Symmetrical Bodies

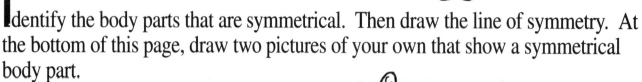

Name _____

Identify the body parts that are symmetrical. Then draw the line of symmetry. At the bottom of this page, draw two pictures of your own that show a symmetrical body part.

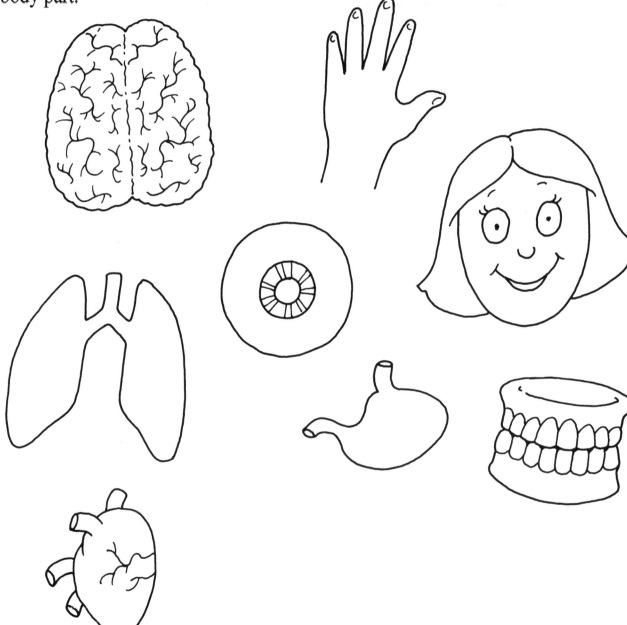

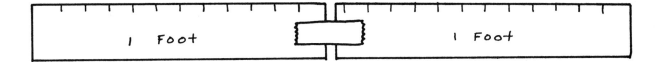

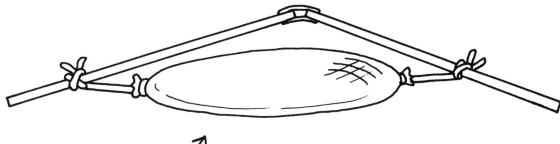

Expanded

Contracted

MATERIALS:

two 12" rulers
masking tape
9" balloon
yarn

DIRECTIONS:

1. Tape two 12" rulers together end-to-end, leaving a space approximately 1/4" wide between them.

2. Blow the balloon about halfway full and knot it. Tie one end of a 6" length of yarn around one end of the balloon. Repeat for the other end.

3. Tie one free end of yarn about 4" from the free end of one ruler. Tie the other free end of yarn about 4" from the free end of the other ruler. Use tape to hold the yarn in place if necessary.

4. This setup can demonstrate to students how our muscles work, particularly in the upper arm. The rulers represent the bones in the arm (the humerus, radius, and ulna). The balloon represents the biceps muscle. When the arm is extended out straight, the muscle moving those bones is expanded. When the arm is bent at the elbow, the muscle is contracted.

5. Ask a volunteer to hold the rulers at either end. When he or she moves the rulers so they are nearly straight, the balloon will expand. When the rulers are moved so they are bent, the balloon will contract.

6. Inform students that muscles usually work in pairs. Ask them to identify the muscle that works with the biceps when the arm is in motion (triceps, located at the back of the upper arm). Ask them to describe what happens to each muscle as the arm is moved (as the biceps expands, the triceps contracts, and vice versa).

29

Reflexes Demonstration

Divide the class into pairs of students. Ask one student in each pair to close his or her eyes for about 1 minute, holding a hand over the closed eyes. When the minute is up, the students with closed eyes may open them and look directly into the eyes of their partner. The partners should be prepared to observe closely what happens when their partners open their eyes.

Have the partners switch roles and compare and contrast the eyes before closing and after opening. Inform the class that the iris contracts and expands in response to light; bright light causes the iris to contract, while dim light causes the iris to expand.

Working in pairs again, ask one student in each pair to sit with one leg crossed over the other so the top leg can swing freely. The other partner should then tap the free leg just below the kneecap with the edge of his or her hand. If the proper place is tapped, the free leg will jerk out.

Another way to demonstrate reflexes is to activate the sneeze reflex. Distribute feathers to several students and have each student tickle the inside of a classmate's nose.

One last easy-to-show reflex is the blinking reflex. Inform students that we blink automatically when our eyes feel dry. We also blink as a protective measure when something comes close to our eyes. Divide the class into pairs. Ask one partner in each pair to hold a 12" x 12" piece of plastic wrap approximately 4" in front of his or her face. Then have the other partner gently throw a crumpled-up piece of paper at the first student's eyes. Almost always, the first student will blink in response to the approach of an object so near the eyes. Have the partners switch roles. Compare and contrast the reactions of the students to the experience.

The Learning Maze

FINISH

Reproduce the maze three times for each student. Staple each set together and distribute to the class. Divide the class into pairs and have each pair decide which partner will complete the maze first.

Inform the pairs that as the first partner does the maze three times in succession, the other partner will time him or her. When the first partner has completed the maze three times, have partners switch roles.

Compare and contrast finishing times for the first, second, and third trials. Discuss which took the longest and which took the shortest time. Did the time to complete the maze decrease from the first trial to the last? Why do students think they got these results? Ask students how they felt as they worked on each maze.

31

Learning by Memorization

Explain to the class that one of the ways in which humans learn is by memorization: studying something over and over until it is stored in the memory. Then give the students the two lists below to memorize. Tell them they will have 5 minutes to memorize the words in each list.

of	lion
under	tree
napkin	phone
carpet	windmill
encyclopedia	baton
flowers	umbrella
bulldozer	acorn
refrigerator	envelope

After the 5 minutes are up, ask students to write the words on another sheet of paper. Have students check the lists of words to see who was able to memorize the words and rewrite them with the fewest mistakes.

Ask students to explain any memorization techniques they have to the rest of the class.

Next, ask children to try to memorize the two lists below. See which students are able to memorize these lists in the proper order and how (the list of words forming a sentence should be easier and cause fewer mistakes).

duck	seeing
train	him
chair	once
paper	more
frame	made
basket	me
mattress	very
backpack	happy

Another demonstration takes into consideration distractions that may occur while the students are trying to learn. As children memorize the following two lists of words and then write them on another sheet of paper, play loud music or make some noise with a ruler or bell.

place mat	jeans
string	elevator
bookmark	snow
shovel	doorknob
ribbon	doll
wire	apartment
shelves	clothesline
fingernail	hat rack

See which students can perform the task with the fewest mistakes and ask them how they are able to memorize with the distractions. List student responses on the board and discuss how other students may be able to use these methods when studying.

Brainy Thoughts

Explain to the class that the brain is the most complicated—and important—organ in the human body. Tell students that doctors and research scientists are constantly finding out more and more information about this complex subject.

Ask if anyone can explain briefly how the brain works. The brain is made up of billions of nerve cells. It controls all bodily activity. Nerves carry messages from the sense organs to the brain. The brain sends messages as well as receives them; for example, it controls breathing, heart rhythm, and balance.

Tell students that there are three main parts to the brain. Draw a simple diagram on the blackboard or a large piece of oaktag to illustrate:

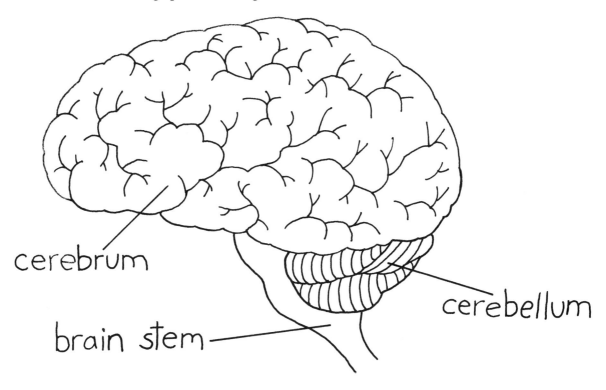

cerebrum

cerebellum

brain stem

The **cerebrum** is the largest part of the brain. It is responsible for receiving messages from the sense organs and sending out nerve impulses that control movement. The computer-like part of the human brain that stores information and processes all thoughts is also located in the cerebrum.

The **cerebellum** controls balance and coordination. The cerebellum has a right hemisphere and a left hemisphere. The right hemisphere of the cerebellum connects via nerves to the left side of the body; the left hemisphere connects to the right side of the body.

The **brain stem** connects the cerebrum to the spinal cord and contains the **medulla**, which controls breathing, heart rate, and other vital functions.

After discussing the brain and how it works, ask each child to research one bodily function and explain step-by-step how the brain controls it. For example, a student might wish to explain how the body perceives a candy bar as tasting sweet, or how exercise accelerates one's heart rate. Encourage students to share their research with the rest of the class.

How Do I Get to Room 102?

Name _____

Answer the following questions by looking at the map of the first floor of a small hospital.

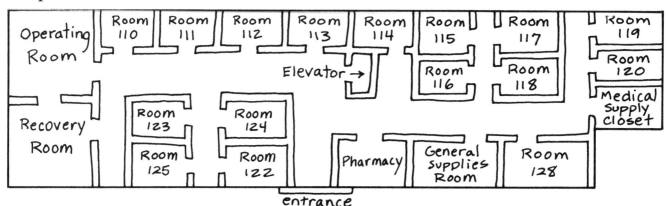

1. You are supposed to meet your ride home at the elevator. You are visiting your sister in Room 117. How will you get to the elevator? _____

_____

2. A patient in Room 123 needs his medication. How will you get to the pharmacy? _____

_____

3. The child in Room 110 just spilled his juice. You need new sheets, pajamas, and a blanket from the general supplies room. Which way will you go? _____

_____

4. A girl is visiting a sick friend in Room 116 and will then go to the recovery room to see her mother, who is a nurse. She is already 5 minutes late. What route should she take to get to the recovery room? _____

_____

5. The operating room is short on medical gowns, gloves, and face masks. An operation is scheduled for 8:00 a.m., and all the supplies must be in place before the surgeon arrives. How would you get to the medical supply closet from the operating room? _____

_____

A Cell Model

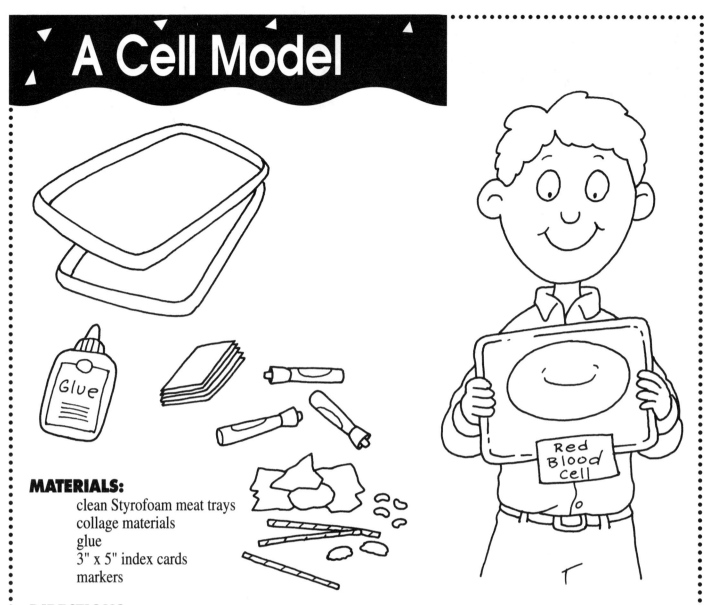

MATERIALS:

clean Styrofoam meat trays
collage materials
glue
3" x 5" index cards
markers

DIRECTIONS::

1. Discuss some basic facts about cells with the class, such as:

> Cells are the basic units of life in our bodies.
> Every part of a human body is made up of cells.
> There are different types and shapes of cells.
> Cells have different functions.

2. Ask students to explain the function of nerve cells, muscle cells, and bone cells. Although these cells and others in the body have different functions, most cells have the same things in common. A basic cell consists of a cell membrane, cytoplasm, the endoplasmic reticulum, and organelles such as the nucleus, nucleoli, ribosomes, lysosomes, Golgi apparatuses, centrioles, and mitochondria. Each organelle has a different function to perform in the cell.

3. From the school library or a science teacher, borrow books that show representations and actual photographs of cells of different shapes, sizes, and types. Research what it is each cell contains within its membrane.

4. Distribute one meat tray to each student. Arrange a collection of collage materials and glue at each table. Have students make models of a basic cell, using the tray as the cell membrane and cytoplasm and manipulating the collage materials into the shapes and sizes of various organelles. For example, pipe cleaners may be twisted and cut down to size to resemble mitochondria or Golgi apparatuses. The ribosomes may be fabric scraps cut into small circles, or small beans.

5. Have students label the cells when they are finished, using index cards cut into 1" x 3" strips. Students may wish to name the function of their cell also, such as a "red blood cell." They may then write a short paragraph describing the work a red blood cell does and attach it to their cell.

6. Display students' cells on a classroom bulletin board or in the hallway for everyone to see.

Jumble and Match

Name _____

Unscramble the names of the following words about blood and then match them to the correct definition.

a. pialrsceali _____

b. maslap _____

c. snevi _____

d. dre lobod lecls _____

e. tellapets _____

f. slupe _____

g. cleekouty _____

h. wrarom _____

i. treirase _____

j. bloomhegin _____

1. a protein containing iron; found in red blood cells

2. very thin blood vessels joining small arteries to small veins

3. cells in blood carrying oxygen and carbon dioxide

4. a white blood cell

5. a substance inside bones that manufactures red blood cells

6. the liquid part of blood

7. pieces of cells; necessary for blood clotting

8. blood vessels carrying blood away from the heart

9. blood vessel carrying blood to the heart

10. the rate at which the heart beats

Mouth Maps

MATERIALS:

    crayons or markers
    oaktag
    old magazines or workbooks
    glue
    scissors
    folders with pockets

DIRECTIONS:

1. Ask the class to guess how many teeth are found in a healthy mouth. Take all guesses, then inform the class that 32 is the normal number. Tell students that they probably have only 28 teeth because their wisdom teeth have not yet come in. (This usually occurs between the ages of 18 and 25).

2. Ask students to identify the four different types of teeth found in the human mouth and encourage them to explain what the function of each type of tooth is. Explain that the incisors (8) are used for cutting; the canines (4) are used for cutting, piercing, and holding foods; the premolars (8) are used for tearing as well as grinding; and the molars (12) are used for grinding and stabilization of the tooth and jaw relationships.

3. To make the puzzle, reproduce the art on page 38 once for each student. Students may decorate their teeth patterns any way they like with crayons or markers, or leave them white.

4. Glue the teeth patterns onto similar-sized pieces of oaktag.

5. Ask students to look for interesting pictures in old magazines or workbooks. Glue one picture to the other side of each piece of oaktag.

6. Tell students to cut the teeth picture apart along the dotted lines and mix up the pieces.

7. Ask the class to reassemble their teeth puzzles inside a file folder. Then tell each child to close the front file cover, flip the folder over onto its back, and open the back cover. If the picture fits together correctly, the teeth puzzle was also done correctly.

8. Have each child store his or her teeth puzzle parts in the file folder.

Mouth Maps

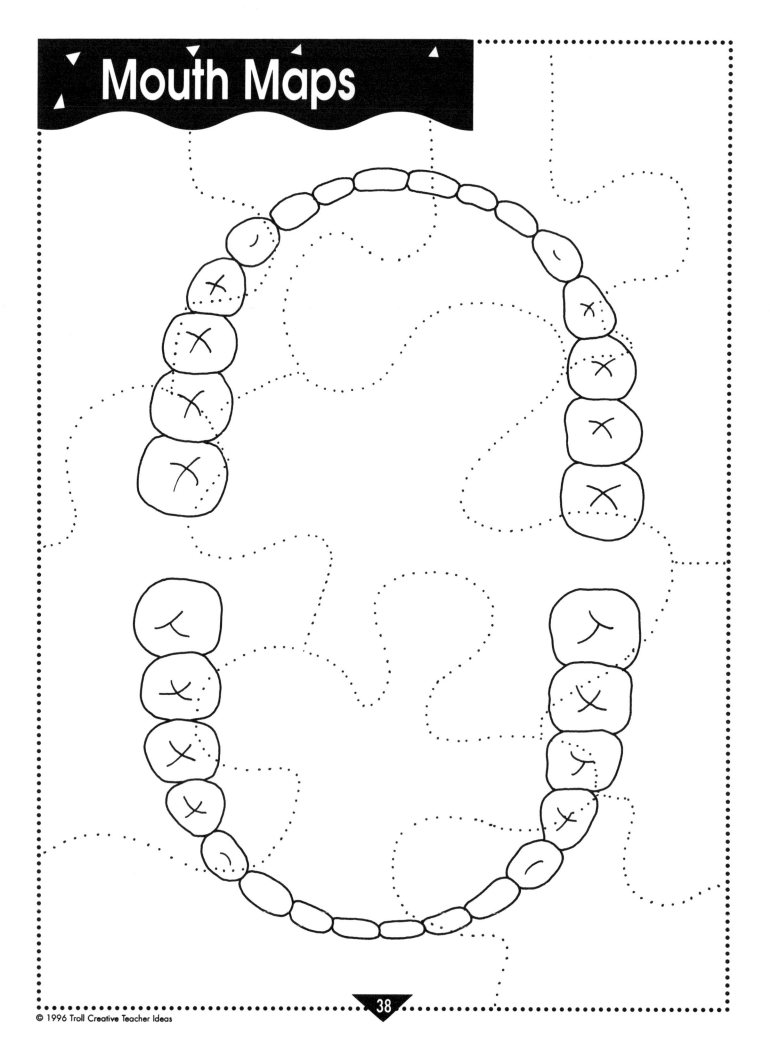

In Case of Emergency

Name _____

In an emergency: **Keep calm.**
Use your common sense.
Think things through and do them one at a time.
Remember that people are more important than things.

In order to be useful in an emergency, you must keep your head clear and not panic. Think before you act, and then do what is necessary in logical order. Remember, never put yourself in danger in order to rescue an animal or object.

Keep this list of numbers by the phone in case of emergency.

Fire:

_____

Police:

_____

Doctor:

_____

Nearest emergency hospital:

_____

Poison control center:

_____

Family member to be called in case of emergency:

_____

Neighbor to be called in case of emergency:

_____

How Do You Feel About It?

Yuck!

Name _____

Write down the emotions you feel when reading the captions on the boxes below. You may wish to draw a picture or write a short poem if you feel more comfortable expressing yourself that way. Share your responses with a small group of your classmates. Did anyone else feel the same as you? Differently than you? Find out why, and try some of your classmates' ideas to brighten your mood next time you need a boost.

dentist	hospital	nutrition
alcohol	pollution	smoking

MATERIALS:

crayons or markers
construction paper
old magazines or workbooks
scissors
collage materials
glue
hole punchers
thread or yarn
2" x 12" strips of oaktag

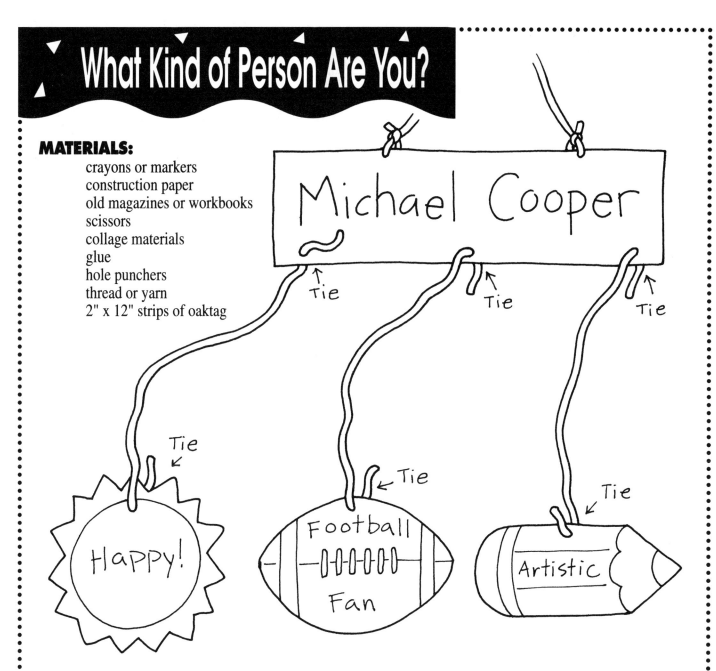

DIRECTIONS:

1. Give each student time to respond to the following questions: What do you like about yourself? What don't you like about yourself? What do you like to do? What don't you like to do? What is your favorite place? What do you want to do when you are an adult? Pick three words to describe yourself.

2. Distribute the materials for students to make mobiles based on the information they provided to the questions above. On construction paper, students may draw pictures or write words, poems, or short stories to illustrate who they are. They may also wish to incorporate magazine pictures into their mobiles.

3. Students may also make more abstract additions to their mobiles by creating illustrations of their emotions or attitudes. For this, varied colors, shapes, and shape

sizes may be important.

4. Tell children to punch a hole in the top of each illustration and make a line of holes close to one long edge of their oaktag strips. Tie one end of a length of thread or yarn to each illustration. (Yarn lengths may be different or similar based on student's preference.)

5. Tie the other end of the yarn into a hole along the strip of oaktag. Tell students to write their names along the oaktag strips. Mobiles may be hung from the lights or ceiling with more thread or yarn.

6. Allow time for the class to browse through the mobiles. Hold a question-and-answer session in which students may offer comments or ask questions about the mobiles.

School Checkup Time

Name _____

Read the statistics on some of the students in Ms. Piper's class of 11-year-olds. Then answer the questions based on that information.

STUDENT'S NAME	HEIGHT	WEIGHT
Benny	4'3"	51 lbs.
Sara	4'8"	62 ½ lbs.
Craig	5'0"	75 ¼ lbs.
Missy	4'9"	60 ½ lbs.
Julie	5'0"	82 ¾ lbs.
Max	5'2"	87 ½ lbs.

1. How much less does Sara weigh than Max? _____

2. Whose height totals 56 inches? 60 inches? _____

3. Whose height in inches equals his or her weight in pounds? _____

4. Which two students' heights together equal 9'? _____

   _____

5. Who is six inches taller than Sara? _____

6. If Missy grows 4" next year, how tall will she be? _____

7. Max's wrestling match next week is with an 89-pound boy. How much weight will Max have to gain if he wants to weigh in at the same weight? _____

8. Make up a question on your own for a classmate to answer.

Going Shopping

MATERIALS:

clean food boxes and containers
crayons or markers
5" x 7" index cards
12" x 18" construction paper
play money: bills and coins

DIRECTIONS:

1. Ask for donations of clean grocery food boxes and containers from the class and friends. Catergorize the containers according to usage or food group. Then arrange them on tables in the classroom to resemble a grocery store.

2. Have a group design name signs for the store. Price tags must also be made for each item. Students should decide on realistic prices before attaching the tags.

3. The last group of signs to be made will be the reduced-price signs. Create signs that show "1/3 off," "50% off," "25% off," "1/4 off," and so on.

4. Attach the signs to the tables and to the food containers if necessary.

5. Ask one group of students to be the shoppers. Distribute the play money to these students. Ask another group of students to be the cashiers at the different tables. Give the cashiers some play money to use to make change.

6. Allow students 5 minutes to browse through the merchandise and make a shopping list showing items they would like to purchase. This time can also be used by the cashiers to look through what is on their tables and see what the discount is for their products.

7. When the shoppers have made their lists, they should figure out how much their items cost with the discount, and then approach the cashier with their purchases. Cashiers must be ready to check the calculations of their customers and to give change.

8. One student may be selected to play the manager in case of disagreements over discounts or change. When everyone has had a chance to shop, students may switch roles and begin again. (If students are shoppers twice, they should choose new items and discount tables.)

Mystery Personalities

MATERIALS:

large box with lid
construction paper
scissors
glue
collage materials

DIRECTIONS:

1. Find an old but sturdy box and cover the outside and lid with construction paper. Ask each student to donate 10 minutes to decorate a portion of the box. What they create should reflect some aspect of their personalities.

2. Ask each student to bring in some items that also reflect his or her personality, such as a cassette tape, a piece of clothing, a photograph or drawing, a favorite object, a lucky object, a favorite book or magazine, or anything else that will represent who the student is.

3. Have students add their items to the box over the course of several days without allowing other students to see what they are adding. Keep a list of items brought in by the students for easy identification when the activity is done.

4. For the first activity, ask a student to come to the box and pick out all the items that seem to belong to one personality. For example, he or she may pick out a baseball, a picture of a famous sports figure, and a

sports book. These items might represent someone with a love for sports, the outdoors, and fitness. When the student is done creating a personality category, ask him or her to explain what type of personality is represented by the objects. Continue creating personality categories with other student volunteers.

5. Another activity to do with the class is to hold up one item and ask the students to give their opinions about what type of a person is likely to treasure that item. Continue the activity, choosing one item from each student. Write down students' responses to the items. Then ask the students to come forward, claim their items, and place them on their desks.

6. Go around the room asking students to reveal whether they were surprised to see some of the items that are owned and liked by their classmates. Ask questions, such as, "Were you surprised to learn that Juan likes music?" or "How many of you knew that Sam is interested in martial arts?

44

Information Posters

MATERIALS:

crayons or markers
poster-sized paper
paints and brushes
collage materials
glue
old magazines and workbooks

DIRECTIONS:

1. Brainstorm with the class about the types of things they think might be dangerous to their health. With the class's help, categorize their thoughts. Some suggestions are: pollution, smoking, drugs, alcohol, peer pressure, and guns. Have students borrow books from the library to research the dangers these things can cause.

2. Distribute the poster materials to each table. Ask the class to create posters that will warn their schoolmates of the dangers of these substances and circumstances.

3. Encourage children to add sections to their posters with positive messages for the readers that might help them decide against becoming involved with drugs or alcohol. A slogan might be, "You've got a lot to give! Don't blow it all on cigarettes."

4. Create a gallery of the class's posters and allow them time to walk around viewing their classmates' work. Discuss the messages on the posters and what age range or group they are targeting. Get permission to hang the posters in a hallway or showcase for all to learn valuable lessons about the dangers of certain substances.

5. A follow-up might be to go into other classrooms with the messages of prevention. Students may wish to create their own ways of presenting their information. Children may wish to present short plays or puppet skits, sing songs, write poems, make videos, or perform dances.

45

Create a Creature

MATERIALS:

clean garbage
empty spools
paper clips
string or yarn
straws
jar lids
collage materials
wheels
handles
glue
tape
scissors

DIRECTIONS:

1. Brainstorm with the class about what makes a person. Is it personality? Looks? Intelligence? The way a person moves? Talks? Sings? Ask students for words we use to describe a person.

2. Inform students that they will be creating their own creatures, ones that will have pasts and futures. Before beginning, or as they create, each student must think up a culture from which his or her creature comes. Each child must tell how the creature gets nourishment, and describe a body part that takes in that nourishment. The creature must be able to move and communicate, and it must have some sort of protective device to enable it to survive.

3. Distribute the materials to the class and allow students some time each day to work on their creatures. They may also wish to go to the library to do some research on specific places, cultures, animals, people, or languages.

4. When the creatures are completed, remind the class of the criteria needed for presentation: culture, food, movement, communication, and protection. Students may also want to add whether their creatures are male, female or androgenous, and what their names are. Each student should write his or her creature's story on a sheet of paper decorated to reflect the creature's culture or purpose. Share the creatures with other classes and put them on display along with the students' creature descriptions.

Scavenger Hunt

Group Name

Divide into groups with equal numbers of students to look for the items listed below. The first group to collect all the items on the list is the winner.

- a news story about medical care
- something people use in order to see better
- a medical or dental tool (can be a toy)
- one item from each of the five food groups
- the name of the first woman doctor
- the name and date of the last immunization you received
- a picture of someone happy
- a bone
- something a baby would use, something an adult would use, something an elderly person would use
- something that makes a high-pitched sound
- clothing for each season: summer, fall, winter, spring
- the phone number for the fire station and the police station nearest your school
- five reasons not to take drugs
- a list of things that should be in a first aid kit
- the word *doctor* in five different languages

Can You Guess What It Is?

Read the story *Seven Blind Mice*, by Ed Young, to the class. Discuss the moral with students. Ask if anyone has had the experience in their lives of jumping to conclusions based only on partial information, and ask what the consequences were.

Collect a box full of objects with which the students may or may not be familiar. Keep the box covered so students will not know what is inside it. Call two students to the front of the room. Have them sit in chairs close together. Blindfold them.

Inform the two students that you will be giving them an object to touch. They may only touch their side of the object. When they are both done feeling, on the count of three, ask the students to make guesses about the identity of the object.

When the guesses have been made, the students may take off their blindfolds and check their answers. Call up other pairs of students to try their skills at guessing the identity of other objects in the box.

Is it a Teddy Bear?

The Incredible Me

Name _____

You have many roles that you play in life, such as male or female, student, and child. Write all the words you can think of that name the many different roles you have every day.

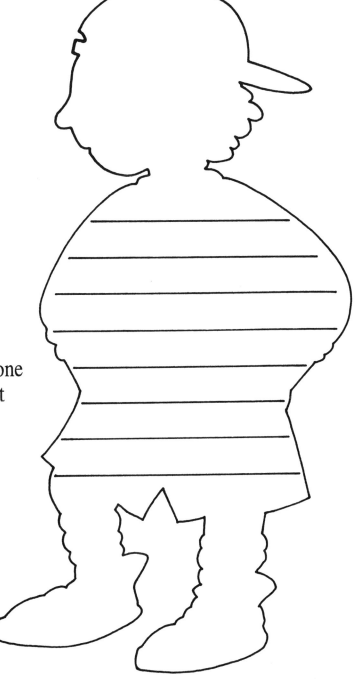

On the back of this page, write a short story or a poem about someone whom the words at the right might describe.

On Your Own

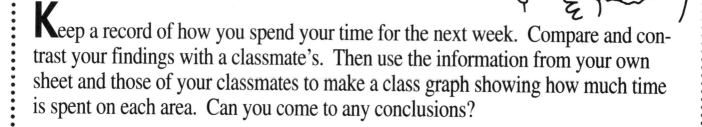

Too much time on homework!

Name _____

Keep a record of how you spend your time for the next week. Compare and contrast your findings with a classmate's. Then use the information from your own sheet and those of your classmates to make a class graph showing how much time is spent on each area. Can you come to any conclusions?

	TV	Homework	After-School	Work	Sleep	Family	Friends	Activities
Mon.								
Tues.								
Wed.								
Thurs.								
Fri.								
Sat.								
Sun.								

Blueberry Muffins

Help students make this delicious snack to enjoy as an afternoon treat!

MATERIALS:

3 1/2 cups sifted flour
1 cup sugar
5 teaspoons baking powder
1 1/2 teaspoons salt
2 well-beaten eggs
1 1/2 cups milk
2/3 cup salad oil
2 cups fresh or well-drained frozen blueberries

DIRECTIONS:

1. Sift together the flour, sugar, baking powder, and salt. Make a well in the center.
2. Combine the eggs, milk, and salad oil together in a small bowl. Then pour into the dry ingredients.
3. Stir quickly, but only until the dry ingredients are moistened.
4. Gently stir in the blueberries.
5. Fill greased muffin pans or muffin paper cups one-half to two-thirds full.
6. Bake at 400°F for about 25 minutes. Makes approximately 24 muffins.

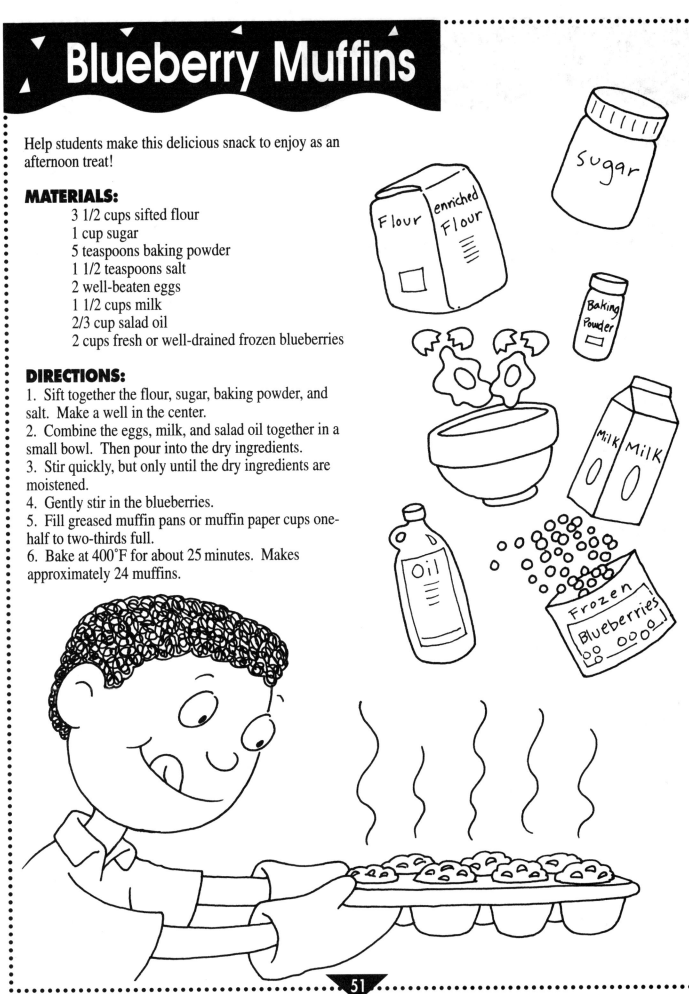

51

All Systems Go!

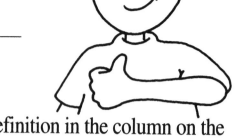

Name _____

Match each system in the column on the left to its definition in the column on the right.

1. Muscular

2. Circulatory

3. Endocrine

4. Reproductive

5. Skeletal

6. Excretory

7. Digestive

8. Nervous

9. Skin

10. Respiratory

A. Supports and protects the body

B. Produces eggs in females and sperm in males

C. Breaks down food

D. Covers and protects the body

E. Supports the body and allows it to move

F. Carries messages from the brain throughout the body

G. Controls metabolism

H. Removes waste from the body

I. Supplies oxygen and removes carbon dioxide from the body

J. Carries food, oxygen, and waste throughout the body

Parts of the Ear

Name _____

Label each part of the ear on the lines provided. Then describe the role of each part in hearing.

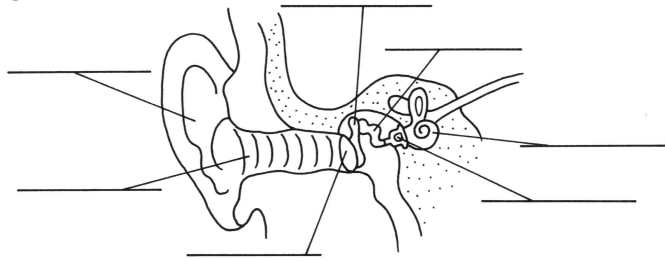

outer ear _____

_____

hammer _____

_____

anvil _____

_____

auditory canal _____

_____

eardrum _____

_____

stirrup _____

_____

cochlea _____

_____

Parts of the Eye

Name _____

Label each part of the eye on the lines provided. Then describe the role of each part in sight.

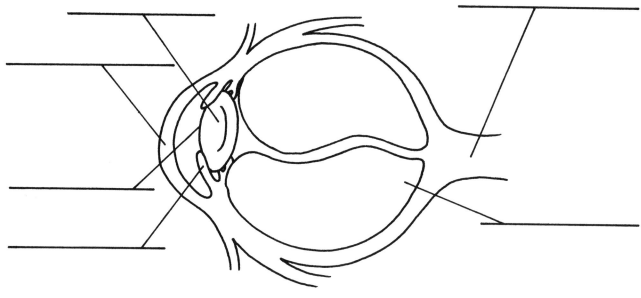

iris _____

_____

pupil _____

_____

cornea _____

_____

lens _____

_____

optic nerve _____

_____

retina _____

_____

Parts of a Cell

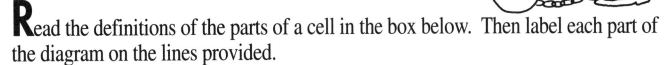

Name _____

Read the definitions of the parts of a cell in the box below. Then label each part of the diagram on the lines provided.

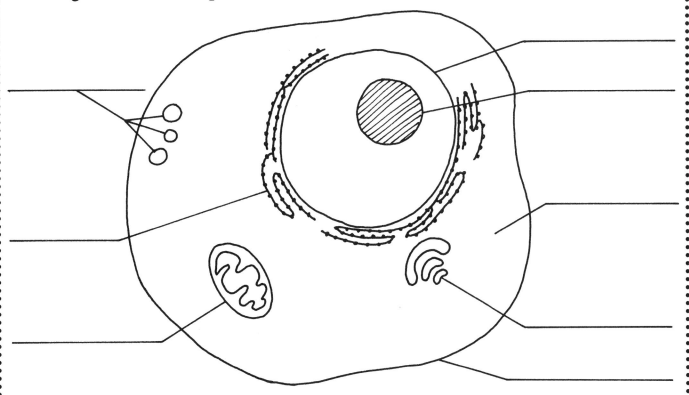

cell membrane—the outer wall of a cell

nucleus—part of a cell that contains the genes

mitochondria—the "engine" of a cell; contains enzymes responsible for the conversion of food to energy

cytoplasm—the fluid (protoplasm) inside a cell

nucleolus—a small part of the nucleus that contains protein and RNA (ribonucleic acid)

Golgi apparatus—machinery for protein transport

vacuole—a small space in the protoplasm of a cell

endoplasmic reticulum—protein-making machinery

Name That Cell!

Name _____

The cells in our bodies have many different shapes. These shapes help cells perform different functions. For example, nerve cells have long parts called axons that help send signals from one part of the body to the brain. Red bloods cells have a "doughnut" shape that allows the cells to change shape when passing through narrow blood vessels called capillaries.

Using the words in the box, identify each of the types of cells shown below. Then write a sentence that tells how the shape of each cell helps it to perform its function. If you need help, use an encyclopedia.

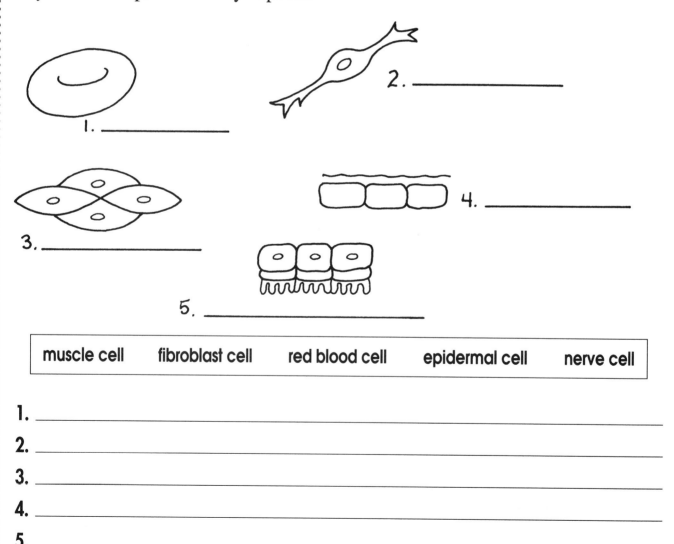

1. _____

2. _____

3. _____

4. _____

5. _____

| muscle cell | fibroblast cell | red blood cell | epidermal cell | nerve cell |

1. _____
2. _____
3. _____
4. _____
5. _____

Straw Test

Explain to students what happens when blood vessels become constricted by arteriosclerosis, a chronic disease in which the thickening and hardening of the walls of arteries causes reduced blood flow. Tell the class that when a blood clot forms inside the body, it may become caught in a constricted blood vessel. This may cause heart failure, a stroke, a lung embolism, and/or organ failure.

To illustrate how this happens, have a volunteer draw water through a drinking straw. Then have the volunteer slowly constrict the straw while sucking on it. What happens? (It becomes more difficult to draw water through the straw.) Ask the volunteer to tell what happens when the straw is almost completely closed. (It requires a great deal of effort to draw water through the smaller opening.)

Ask students what might occur when a blood vessel becomes constricted. Explain that reduced blood flow may cause organs to deteriorate, reduce the efficiency of a particular system in the body, reduce the amount of oxygen and nutrients carried throughout the body, and so on. Tell the class that the increased amount of work required to pump blood through the body appears as high blood pressure.

If possible, invite the school nurse or a local nurse or doctor to come to the classroom to talk about the causes of arteriosclerosis. Later, make a list with the class of healthful foods and activities that help prevent this disease.

The Leg Bone's Connected to . . .

Name _____

Look at the picture of the skeleton below. On the lines provided, write in the name of each bone. Use an encyclopedia or health book for reference.

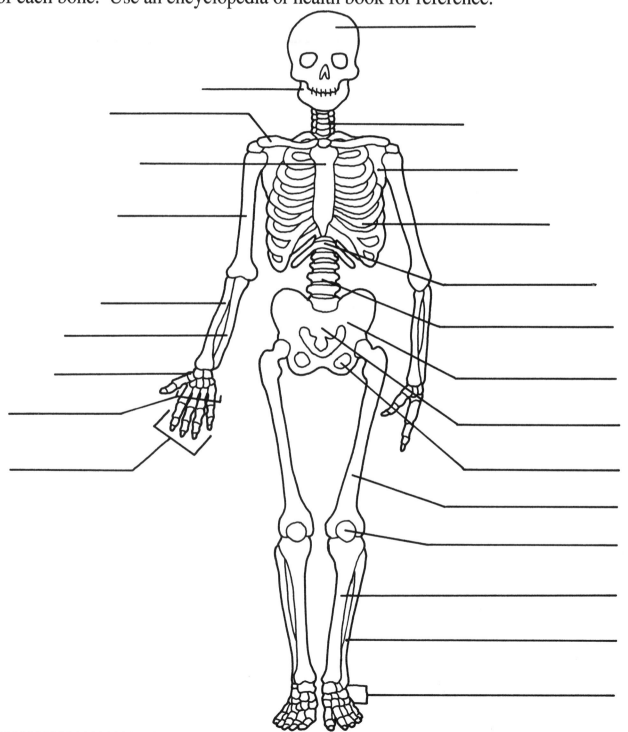

How Many Did You Say?

Name _____

Read each of the questions below. Then choose one of the numbers in the box to give an approximate or exact answer to each question. Use an encyclopedia or health book for reference.

1. About how many times a day does your heart beat? _____

2. How many chambers are in your heart? _____

3. How many teeth does the average adult have? _____

4. How many pounds does your brain weigh? _____

5. How many bones are in the human body? _____

6. How many calories should the average 10-year-old consume in a day? _____

7. How many bones are in one human foot? _____

8. How many bones are there in one human hand? _____

9. About how many of your cells wear out and are replaced each day? _____

10. About how long are the intestines in the human body (in feet)? _____

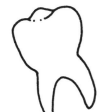

206	27	4	28
1,500	32	26	3
100,000	2,000,000,000		

Skeletal System Game

MATERIALS:

- scissors
- glue
- large piece of construction paper
- oaktag
- clear contact paper (optional)

DIRECTIONS:

1. Reproduce the skeleton patterns on pages 61–62 two times. Cut out around each skeleton and glue the pieces together on a large piece of construction paper.
2. Reproduce the game cards on pages 63–64 two times and cut them out.
3. Write a question about the human body on the back of each card. Write each answer on the front (printed side) of the card. Some suggested questions:

   What is the central mass of a cell called? (nucleus)
   Food travels from your mouth to your stomach through this organ. (esophagus)
   Which organ contains four chambers? (heart)
   What carries blood away from the heart? (arteries)
   Where is the retina located? (eye)
   What is another name for epidermis? (skin)

4. Mount the cards on oaktag. Laminate if desired.

HOW TO PLAY:

(for two players)
1. Give each player a skeleton game board. Place the game cards in a stack in the middle of the playing surface.
2. Provide the players with crayons or markers. Have students flip a coin to see who goes first.
3. The first player draws a card and reads the question. The player must try to answer the question correctly, then turn the card over to see if he or she is correct.
4. If the player is correct, he or she should follow the directions on the card and color in part of his or her skeleton (or the other player's skeleton). If the player is incorrect, he or she may not follow the directions on the card.
5. The next player goes. Play continues until one of the players has colored in all the bones in his or her skeleton.

Skeletal System Game

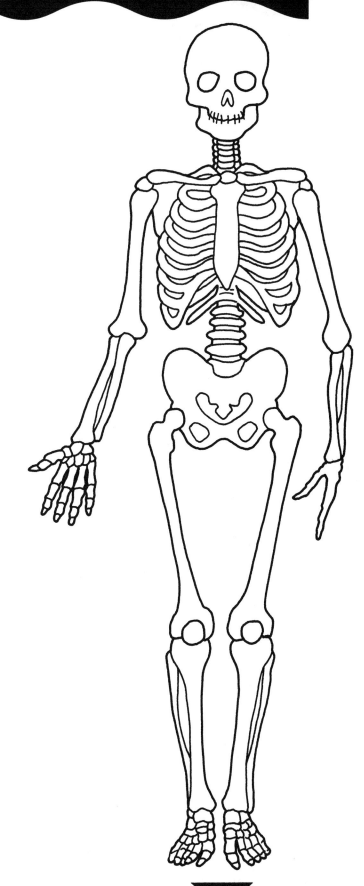

Skeletal System Game

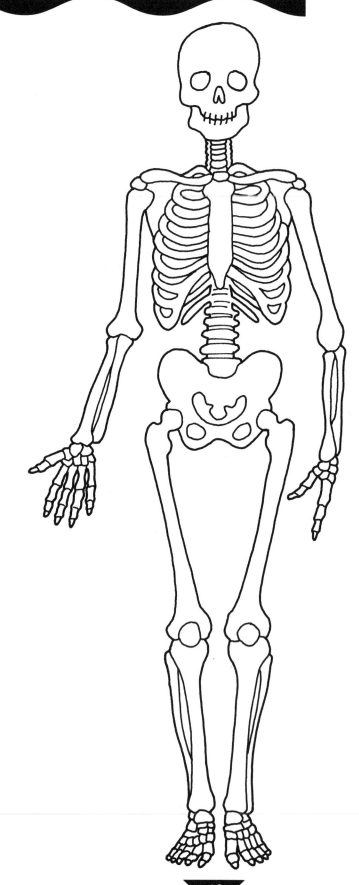

Skeletal System Game

Color in the Phalanges	Color in the Pelvis	Color in the Femur
Color in the Patella	Color in the Fibula	Color in the Tibia
Color in the Tarsals	Color Any Part	Color Any Part
Color Any Part	Color in one part of another player's skeleton	Color in one part of another player's skeleton

Skeletal System Game

Color in the Cranium

Color in the Maxilla

Color in the Mandible

Color in the Clavicle

Color in the Scapula

Color in the Sternum

Color in the Ribs

Color in the Humerus

Color in the Vertebrae

Color in the Radius

Color in the Ulna

Color in the Carpals

Where Does the Food Go?

Have a class discussion about the ways foods break down in the human body. Tell students that the food we eat provides important nutrients. Nutrients provide the raw materials for the tissue in human bodies, and they also provide energy.

On a large piece of oaktag, design a chart like the one on this page. If desired, ask volunteers to help fill in the chart with any information they know.

FOOD	NUTRIENT	EXPLANATION
meat, beans, dairy	amino acids	Amino acids are the subunits of proteins, which are important parts of cells.
fruit, sweets, bread, pasta	glucose	Glucose is converted to energy that the mitochondria of a cell can use.
butter, dairy	cholesterol	Cholesterol is used to make hormones called steroids.
fats, oils	fatty acids	Fatty acids make up cell membranes.
meat, leafy vegetables	iron	Iron is important in cell metabolism and helps the hemoglobin in red blood cells carry oxygen.
fruits, vegetables	vitamins	Vitamins help cells perform their activities.

Divide the class into six groups. Assign each group a specific nutrient to research. Encourage students to use encyclopedias, books about the human body, and other reference materials. If desired, invite a scientist or doctor to the class to help explain the roles nutrients play in the human body.

Best Books About Your Body

Place some or all of the following books in the classroom science or reading center during study units on health and the human body. Encourage students to use the books as reference guides when researching various topics in these fields.

Health and Hygiene by Rae Bains (Troll, 1985)

The Human Body by Gilda Berger (Doubleday, 1989)

The Human Body by Ruth Dowling Bruun and Bertel Bruun (Random House, 1982)

The Macmillan Book of the Human Body by Mary Elting (Macmillan, 1986)

Can You Get Warts from Touching Toads? by Peter Rowan (Messner, 1987)

Why Does My Nose Run? And Other Questions Kids Ask About Their Bodies by Joanne Settel and Nancy Baggett (Macmillan, 1985)

Heartbeats: Your Body, Your Heart by Alvin Silverstein and Virginia B. Silverstein (HarperCollins, 1983)

Body Sense, Body Nonsense by Seymour Simon (HarperCollins, 1981)

Your Body: Muscles and Movement by Gwynne Vevers (Lothrop, 1984)

The Lungs and Breathing by Steve Parker (Franklin Watts, 1989)

The Human Body by Joan Western and Ronald Wilson (Troll, 1991)

Your Body and How It Works by Ovid K. Wong (Childrens Press, 1986)

Unhealthful Addictions

Washington School presents: THE DANGERS OF SMOKING

Smoker

Lead a class discussion about the dangers of alcohol, smoking, and drug abuse. Ask if anyone can explain what an addiction is. Explain to students that certain chemicals, such as the nicotine in cigarettes, can become addicting to human beings after a short period of time. The intensity of the addiction depends upon the chemical itself, the amount that is taken in each day, and the duration of the addiction. (For example, a person who has smoked two packs of cigarettes each day for 20 years most likely has a greater addiction than a person who has smoked one cigarette a day for a week.)

Divide the class into groups of four or five students each. Assign an addiction topic to each group, such as cocaine, alcohol, or heroin. Ask the students in each group to work together to gather as much information as they can about their topic. Then have each group write a skit that they will perform in front of the class (and invited guests, if desired). The skit should focus on a person who is addicted to the chemical the group has researched. Each student in the group should play a part in the skit (for example, doctors or nurses, counselors, family members, or friends). The skit should contain information about the addiction, and show what it might be like to be a person who is addicted to that chemical.

After all the skits have been performed, ask each student to write an essay or several journal entries in the voice of an addicted person. If possible, ask a community speaker who is recovering from an addiction to talk with students about the problems he or she has faced because of the addiction.

Best Books About Healthful Living

Place some or all of the following books in the classroom science or reading center during study units on the dangers of alcohol, drugs, and smoking. Encourage students to use the books as reference guides when researching various topics in these fields.

Making Up Your Mind About Drugs by Gilda Berger (Dutton, 1988)

Cocaine and Crack by Julian Chomet (Franklin Watts, 1987)

Know About Alcohol by Margaret O. Hyde (McGraw-Hill, 1978)

Know About Smoking by Margaret O. Hyde (Walker, 1990)

Something's Wrong in My House by Katherine Leiner (Franklin Watts, 1988)

You Can Say No to a Drink or a Drug by Susan Newman (Putnam, 1986)

Drugs: What They Are, What They Do by Judith Seixas (Morrow, 1991)

Focus on Cocaine and Crack by Jeffrey Shulman (TFC Books, 1990)

Focus on Drugs and the Brain by David Friedman (TFC Books, 1990)

Focus on Hallucinogens by Jeffrey Shulman (TFC Books, 1990)

Focus on Marijuana by Paula K. Zeller (TFC Books, 1990)

Smoking by Lila Gano (Lucent, 1989)

Drugs and Drug Abuse by Brian Ward (Franklin Watts, 1988)

Cocaine by Geraldine Woods and Harold Woods (Franklin Watts, 1985)

Calorie Count

Name _____

Zelda the Zuggernaut has just landed on Earth from the planet Zog. She is supposed to keep careful records of the different foods she eats while visiting our planet.

Help Zelda figure out how many calories she has eaten by multiplying to find the number of calories and then adding the numbers together to find the total per meal and for the day. Then figure out how many calories *you* consumed yesterday!

Breakfast
_____ 11 fried eggs (85 calories each)

_____ 4 glasses of whole milk (150 calories each)

_____ 14 pieces of toast (60 calories each)

_____ 22 pieces of bacon (75 calories each)

_____ 3 glasses of orange juice (120 calories each)

_____ Total breakfast calories

Lunch
_____ 16 peanut-butter-and-jelly sandwiches (260 calories each)

_____ 3 glasses of chocolate milk (200 calories each)

_____ 9 apples (80 calories each)

_____ 32 oatmeal cookies (50 calories each)

_____ Total lunch calories

Dinner
_____ 17 pieces of chicken (90 calories each)

_____ 8 baked potatoes (150 calories each)

_____ 9 ears of corn (75 calories each)

_____ 12 dinner rolls (60 calories each)

_____ 4 glasses of whole milk (150 calories each)

_____ 4 glasses of water (0 calories each)

_____ 7 bowls of ice cream (350 calories each)

_____ Total dinner calories

_____ How many calories did Zelda consume all day?

My Favorite Foods

Name _____

What are your favorite foods? Do you know what these foods contain? On the lines provided, write down your five favorite foods. Then tell the nutritional information for each food (vitamins, nutrients, protein, grams of fat, calories, etc.).

1. Food: _____

_____

_____

_____

_____

_____

2. Food: _____

_____

_____

_____

_____

_____

3. Food: _____

_____

_____

_____

_____

_____

4. Food: _____

_____

_____

_____

_____

_____

5. Food: _____

_____

_____

_____

_____

_____

Which of your favorite foods provides the most nutritional value? _____

_____ Which provides the least? _____

During a study unit about the five senses, help students try to imagine what it might be like to be without one sense, such as sight or hearing. Ask students to pair up, and blindfold one student in each pair. Have each blindfolded student try to complete a simple classroom task, with his or her partner's help. For example, a blindfolded student may try to wash his or her hands, retrieve an item from his or her desk, hand in a paper to the teacher's desk, write something on the chalkboard, or put on his or her coat. After all the blindfolded students have completed their tasks, have them switch roles with their partners.

Talk about the various feelings students had when they were blindfolded. Point out that it is very different being temporarily blindfolded than permanently blind. What kinds of things about their lives would change if they were blind?

To help students experience what it is like to be deaf, spend an hour or two of classroom time using only sign language to communicate. Reproduce the sign language alphabet on page 72 once for each student.

Distribute the alphabet approximately two weeks before the day you will be using sign language in the classroom. If possible, borrow some sign language books from the school or local library and show students some simple signs.

Set up the rules and discuss the assignment that will be taught before the sign-language-only time begins. Students may write notes or use sign language to communicate, but no speaking should be allowed during this time. Afterward, talk about how it felt to have to use sign language or writing to communicate. Was it frustrating? Was it a relief to be able to talk once again? Again, point out that temporarily communicating the way deaf people must do is much different than doing it permanently. How do students think their lives would change if they were deaf?

If possible, invite a blind person and a deaf person to come in and speak to the class about their experiences. Encourage students to become more aware of the daily demands that must be faced by physically challenged people.

Sign Language Alphabet

Name _____

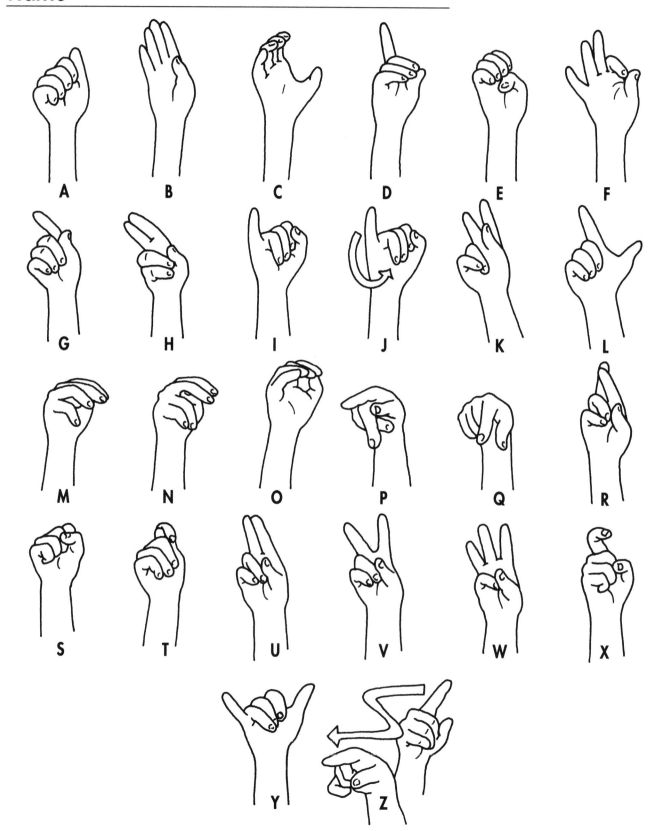

Braille Messages

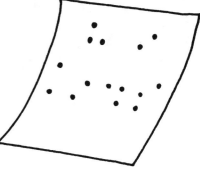

Name _____

The Braille system was invented in 1824 by Louis Braille as a way for blind people to read. Each letter in the Braille alphabet has a different number or arrangement of raised dots. Using their senses of touch, blind people feel the dots on a page to read the letters, words, and sentences that are written down.

Look at the Braille alphabet below. On the lines provided, write a message. Then exchange pages with a classmate and try to decode each other's messages.

a b c d e f g

h i j k l m n

o p q r s t u

v w x y z

_____

_____

_____

First Aid Alert

Name _____

Read each of the paragraphs below. Then, on the lines provided, tell what action should be taken.

1. Jason and Jimmy were playing in the park one day. Jason decided to climb up the slide instead of up the ladder. Jimmy didn't see him and came sliding down. Jason fell off the slide onto the ground. "My arm!" he cried. What should Jimmy do?

_____

_____

2. Lucy and Leigh were walking barefoot by a stream. Suddenly Leigh cried out. She had stepped on some broken glass, and her foot was bleeding hard. What should Lucy do?

_____

_____

3. Tommy and Timmy were making dinner for their family. Tommy took a pot filled with boiling water off the burner and accidentally splashed some of the water on Timmy's hand. What should Tommy do?

_____

_____

4. George and Gina were playing baseball. A gust of wind blew some dirt into Gina's eyes. "I can't see!" she said. "The dirt is stinging my eye!" What should George do?

_____

_____

5. Meg was taking care of her little sister, Molly. Molly began climbing on a pile of wood in the backyard. Suddenly she started screaming. Meg looked up and saw dozens of wasps swarming around Molly. What should Meg do?

_____

_____

Save Me!

Children ages 10 and over can learn lifesaving techniques very readily. Discuss the importance of knowing how to perform cardiopulmonary resuscitation (CPR), which helps restore breathing after someone has suffered cardiac arrest. Ask if anyone knows basic lifesaving skills for swimming or boating emergencies.

Invite a trained lifesaving expert to the class to discuss various lifesaving techniques. Before the expert arrives, discuss what happens when a person goes into cardiac arrest (the heart stops; blood and oxygen flow to the brain are cut off). If any students express an interest in learning more about lifesaving techniques, provide them with the names and locations of local groups (such as the fire station, hospital, and American Red Cross) that sponsor lifesaving classes.

After students have observed the different lifesaving techniques, ask each child to create a lifesaving poster. Encourage students to be creative with their posters, which may feature a slogan (for example, "Stop, Drop, and Roll" for a firefighting poster) or illustrate a lifesaving technique.

If desired, place the posters in the hallway outside the classroom for all to see. Make a banner for the posters entitled, "You Never Know When You Might Need to Save a Life!"

Games from All Over

Help students stay physically and mentally fit by playing some of these games from other cultures.

Tell Me Where (Australia)

Play this game with a small group of students. Choose one student to be "It." Blindfold that player and ask the other students to form a circle around him or her. Place a brick somewhere nearby. Tell the students to try to direct the player who is blindfolded toward the brick. The blindfolded player must listen carefully to the directions, and the other players must be as clear as possible with their instructions. After the player has located the brick, continue playing until everyone has had a turn.

You Dog, You! (Great Britain)

Have all the children line up in a row facing in the same direction. Choose one player to be "It." That player should stand about 20' in front of the line of children. Mark another line 20' beyond the player who is "It." Tell "It" to think of five different kinds of dogs (i.e., beagle, terrier, collie, poodle, and husky) and tell the names to the rest of the class. Each player must silently select one of the dogs. The player who is "It" then calls out the name of one of the dogs. All the children who have chosen that particular dog try to race to the opposite line without being tagged. If a player is tagged by "It," he or she must move to the side and is out of the game. Continue playing until there is only one player left. That player is the new "It" for another round.

Balls in the Circle (New Guinea)

Using chalk, draw a circle about 8' in diameter on a large outdoor surface. Approximately 6' away, at equal distances from the center circle and each other, draw four smaller circles about 3' in diameter. Place five balls in the center circle. Choose four students to play the game. Have each student stand in one of the smaller circles. Tell each player that the object of the game is to get three balls into his or her circle first. Players must pick up the ball from the center circle or another player's circle and put it into his or her own circle. Balls may not be thrown, and only one ball at a time may be picked up. The first student who has three balls in his or her circle is the winner.

Relay Readiness

Play these relay games with the class to help promote physical fitness.

Silly Spoons

Divide the class into groups of five to six students each. Give each student a teaspoon. Ask each group to line up one behind another.

Place a ping pong ball in a small bowl at the front of each line. Have the first player on line spoon the ping pong ball onto his or her spoon, then pass it to the next player on line. Tell students that they may not use their free hands to transfer the ping pong ball.

When the ball has reached the end of each line, that student should go to the front of the line and pass the ball down again. Continue until the student who originally was first in each line returns to that position.

Hoop Relay

Divide the class into two teams. Give each team a large hoop, and have team members line up one behind another.

Place a construction cone about 12' in front of each line. Then place another construction cone 12' beyond the first one. Explain to the class that each player must roll the hoop in a figure eight (to the right of one cone and to the left of the other). When the first player in each line completes the figure eight and returns back to the line, he or she should give the hoop to the next player, then go to the end of the line.

The team whose players complete all their turns first is the winner. For variation, place three (or more) cones in front of each line.

Relay Readiness

Here are some additional relay games that students will enjoy.

Shuttle Race

Divide the class into teams of five to six players each. Have each team line up one in back of another behind a specified line.

Place a small block about 30' in front of each line. Tell the first player in each line to race to the block, pick it up and return to the line as quickly as possible.

That player should hand the block to the next player in line, and then go to the end of the line. The second player takes the block and races down and places the block back in its original position. Then that player runs back to the line and tags the hand of the next player.

Continue playing until everyone in the line has taken a turn and the first player is back at the head of the line.

Locking Arms Relay

Divide the class into groups of six or eight students each. Tell each group to line up one behind another.

The first player in each group must go back-to-back and link arms with the second player in each group. Then the players must move (with linked arms) down to a line about 25' away. When they reach the line, they may unlink their arms. Then the next pair of players continues in the same fashion.

The first team to get all its players across the finish line is the winner.

Cooperative Kids

Play these games of skill involving cooperation and problem-solving techniques.

Untie the Knot

Ask a group of eight volunteers to stand together in an open area. Have children hold hands with the other players until everyone has both hands held. (Make sure that each player is holding the hands of two different people.)

Tell players to try to untie the human knot they have formed. Without letting go hands, have players turn, twist, step over arms, and so on until they have become untied. After the group has unknotted, ask another group of six to come forward and try.

If desired, time each group to see which can untie themselves the fastest.

Team Tag

Begin by choosing two players to be "It." These two players must hold hands, then try to tag the other players in the game. Each time a player is tagged, he or she must join hands and become "It" as well.

When "It" gets to be eight players large, "It" may divide into two groups. Each new group must have at least two players in it. Continue playing tag and making new "Its" until everyone has been tagged.

Endurance Test

31...32...33

Name _____

Practice doing each of the following activities. Then test yourself and measure your performance, filling in the chart below.

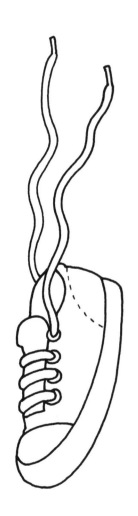
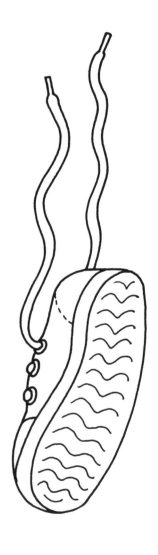

Exercise	# per minute
Sit-ups	
Push-ups	
Jumping jacks	
Touching toes	
Deep knee-bends	
Leg lifts	
Running	**Time**
50 meters	
1/4 mile	
1/2 mile	
1 mile	
Power-walking	**Time**
2 miles	
3 miles	

Fingerprint Fun

MATERIALS:

ink pads
magnifying glasses
glue
construction paper
hole puncher
yarn

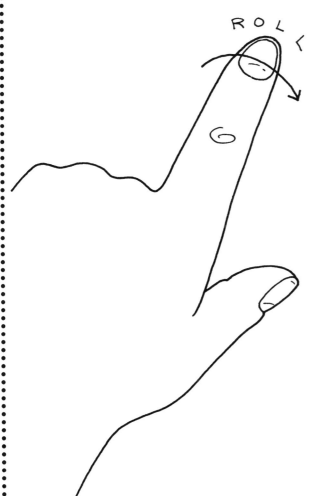

DIRECTIONS:

1. To help students learn about the mystery of finger-prints, make up a class fingerprint book. Before beginning, discuss the three different types of fingerprints (arch, whorl, and loop). Explain that no two finger-prints are exactly alike, which is why people can be identified by their fingerprints.

2. Divide the class into small groups of four or five students each. Provide each group with a small ink pad.

3. Demonstrate to the class how to roll one finger onto the ink pad and then roll (not press) the finger onto a piece of white paper to make a clear fingerprint.

4. Reproduce page 82 once for each child. Have each child fill in the page with his or her fingerprints.

5. Give each group a magnifying glass to use to examine their fingerprints. Encourage students to discuss the different types of fingerprints observed in their groups. If desired, make a graph that shows the total number of arch, whorl, and loop fingerprints in the class.

6. Ask each student to mount his or her fingerprints on a large piece of construction paper. Collect the papers and organize them in a stack to make a class fingerprint book.

7. Make a cover for the book. Punch three holes down the left side of the book, and bind the pages together with yarn. Place the book in the class science center for students to look at during free time.

Fingerprint Fun

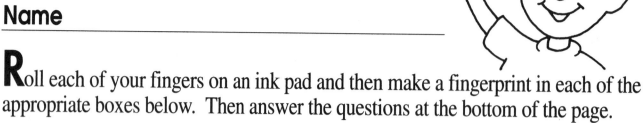

Name

Roll each of your fingers on an ink pad and then make a fingerprint in each of the appropriate boxes below. Then answer the questions at the bottom of the page.

RIGHT HAND

Thumb	Index finger	Middle finger	Ring finger	Little finger

LEFT HAND

Thumb	Index finger	Middle finger	Ring finger	Little finger

Which types of fingerprint patterns do you think you have? Check the chart below and use a magnifying glass to help make your guesses.

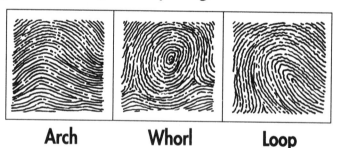

Arch   **Whorl**   **Loop**

	Right hand	Left hand
Thumb		
Index finger		
Middle finger		
Ring finger		
Little finger		

Heart Rate

Name _____

Find your pulse on one of your wrists. Then, use a clock with a second hand to count how many times your pulse beats in a minute. This is your normal heart rate. Perform each of the activities below, then fill in your heart rate. Record the amount of time it takes for your heart rate to return to normal after each activity.

	Beats per minute	Time until normal heart rate returns
Rest		
Run 50 meters		
Wash dishes		
Do 40 jumping jacks		
Do 20 sit-ups		
Clean your room		
Bicycle for 10 minutes		
Run up and down stairs three times		

Which activities cause your heart rate to increase the most? Which activities do not cause a great increase? _____

_____

_____

Why does your heart rate increase when you perform more strenuous activities?

_____

_____

Deep Breaths

MATERIALS:

    clean, empty plastic milk or juice container
    masking tape
    plastic dish pan
    18" plastic tube
    marker

MATERIALS:

1. To illustrate how much air one can breathe into the lungs, set up the following experiment. Fill a clean, empty plastic milk or juice container with water and close it with its cap.

2. Place a strip of masking tape vertically along the side of the container.

3. Fill a plastic dish pan half-full with water. Turn the capped plastic container over and place it upside down in the dish pan. Remove the cap, being careful not to allow air bubbles inside the container.

4. Place one end of an 18" length of plastic tubing inside the milk container. Have a volunteer hold the other end of the tube.

5. Tell the volunteer to take a deep breath and then exhale into the tube. Use a marker to indicate the water level on the strip of masking tape on the container.

6. Explain to students that the amount of air inside the container is the amount of air that was inside the volunteer's lungs. Repeat the experiment, telling student volunteers to take shallow, normal, and deep breaths. Ask students to explain why the water level in the container varies each time.

84

I Can't Do That!

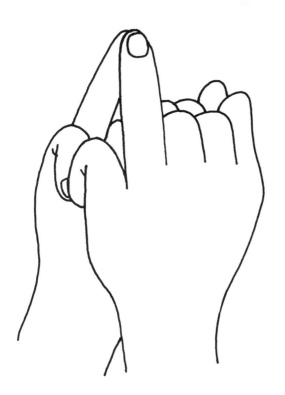

To show students how various parts of their bodies are joined to each other, have the class participate in this experiment. Ask each student to place his or her hands flatly together.

Tell each child to fold down all of his or her fingers except the ring fingers, so that the knuckles are touching, as shown.

Ask each student to try to move one of his or her ring fingers without moving the middle finger, and while keeping the knuckles touching at all times.

Repeat the experiment, using other fingers. What happens?

Explain to the class that the ligaments that attach the middle and ring fingers to each other and to the rest of the hand do not allow for independent movement.

To illustrate the differences in the center of gravity between men's and women's bodies, ask two adult volunteers (one male, one female) to participate in an experiment. Begin by telling each person to stand with the front tips of his or her shoes touching a wall.

Then ask each volunteer to take three steps back from the wall, placing one foot behind another. Place a classroom chair between each volunteer and the wall, with the chair back touching the wall.

Tell the volunteers to lean over and place their heads against the wall. (Their backs should be fairly straight.)

Next, ask each person to try to pick up the chair by the seat, then stand up straight while continuing to hold the chair. Usually, the male volunteer will not be able to stand up straight, but the female will.

Explain to the class that because women have a lower center of gravity, they can lift the chair without losing balance. Since the center of gravity for men is higher (in the torso area), the added weight of the chair causes them to lose their balance. (Note that boys will often be able to perform this activity because their center of gravity has not yet changed.)

Healthful Foods Game

MATERIALS:

crayons or markers
scissors
glue
letter-sized file folder
clear contact paper
envelope
die
4 playing pieces

DIRECTIONS:

1. Reproduce the game board on pages 87–88 once. Color the game board, cut it out, and mount it on the inside of a letter-sized file folder.
2. Reproduce the game cards on page 89 three times. Color the game cards, mount them on oaktag, and laminate. Then cut out the cards.
3. Reproduce the "How to Play" directions on this page once. Cut out the directions and mount them on the outside of the file folder.
4. Provide four playing pieces, such as a penny, nickel, dime, and quarter.
5. Glue an envelope to the back of the file folder. Store the playing pieces, die, and game cards inside the envelope.

HOW TO PLAY:

(for two to four players)
1. Each player rolls the die. The player with the highest number goes first, and play continues clockwise.
2. Players must place their playing pieces on "Start." The first player rolls the die and must move his or her piece clockwise around the board.
3. The player names the food shown on the space he or she has landed on and tells what food group it belongs to. Then he or she takes one of the game cards from that group.
4. The next player goes, and play continues. The object of the game is to collect enough daily servings from each of the five food groups (three servings of dairy foods, three servings from the meats and protein group, three servings of fruit, four servings of vegetables, and eight servings of breads or grains).
5. If a player lands on a space and answers incorrectly or does not need any more servings of that particular food group, he or she does not take a card, and the next player goes.
6. The first player who collects all the necessary servings to complete his or her Food Pyramid is the winner.

Healthful Foods Game

FOOD PYRAMID

START

Healthful Foods Game

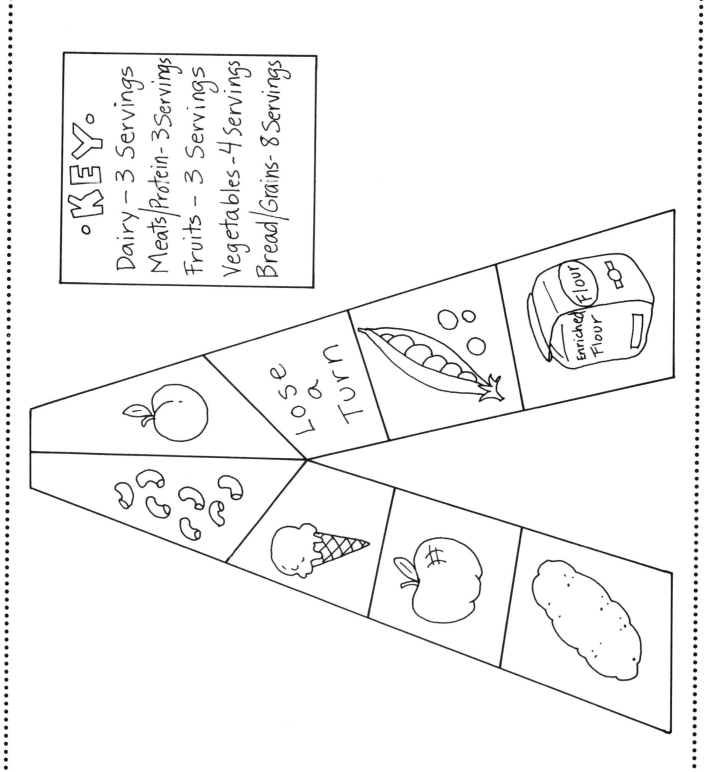

KEY:
Dairy – 3 Servings
Meats/Protein – 3 Servings
Fruits – 3 Servings
Vegetables – 4 Servings
Bread/Grains – 8 Servings

Enriched Flour

Lose a Turn

Healthful Foods Game

Class Garden

Encourage children to become enthusiastic about healthy foods by growing a class garden.

MATERIALS:

    stakes and twine
    potting soil
    vegetable seeds, such as tomato, lettuce,
      cucumbers, pumpkins
    trowels, garden gloves, watering can, plant
      sticks

DIRECTIONS:

1. Ask permission to use a small sunlit area of the school grounds to grow the garden. Have students use trowels to turn the soil over and remove any weeds and rocks.

2. Help students put stakes at the four corners of the garden and wind twine around them to let others know not to step in the garden.

3. Purchase vegetable seeds at a local nursery. Follow planting instructions on the backs of the packets.

4. Each week assign a different student to care for the plants. Have each student gardener report on the garden's progress at the end of his or her week.

5. When the vegetables are ready to harvest, plan a Healthy Foods class party. Make a big salad filled with the vegetables grown in the class garden. If necessary, buy more vegetables at a local farm stand to supplement the salad.

6. Encourage students to participate in preparing and serving the salad. If desired, invite the principal or other school workers. Enjoy!

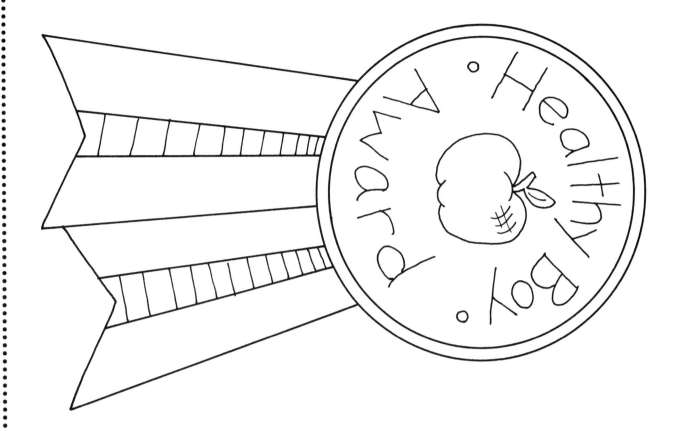

Healthy Kid!

· A W A R D ·

presented to:

for

date

signed

Answers

page 5

Vision—lens, iris, cornea, pupil, retina, optic nerve
Smell—olfactory bulb, nasal passage, olfactory cortex, odors
Taste— epiglottis, trigeminal system, taste buds
Hearing—stirrup, eardrum, auditory canal, hammer, auricle,
                Eustachian tube, cochlea
Touch—Pacinian corpuscles, epidermis, Merkel's disks

page 6

1. CEO
2. EOC
3. OEC
4. ECO
5. COE
6. COE
7. OCE

page 7

1. T Red blood cells carry oxygen to all parts of your body.
2. F The left cerebral hemisphere controls the left side of the body.
3. T Together the brain and spinal cord form the central nervous
        system.
4. F The retina enlarges and contracts to control the amount of light
        passing through the pupil.
5. T The taste buds are located in fungiform papillae on the tongue.
6. F Sound waves strike the cochlea and cause it to vibrate.
7. T Inhaled air goes into the esophagus and the two bronchi.
8. T The larynx is used for speaking, singing, and laughing.
9. F Bile, a digestive juice, is produced by the salivary glands.
10. T There are three types of muscle: smooth, cardiac, and skeletal.

page 8

1 syllable—genes, lungs, lens, brain, nerves, cell, dreams
2 syllables—axon, neuron, pupil, fetus, muscle, synapse, stomach,
                dendrites, mucus, reflex
3 syllables—memory, cerebrum, diaphragm, incisors, cilia, melanin,
                skeleton, emotions, chromosomes, pancreas, aorta
4 syllables—epiglottis, esophagus, alveoli, venae cavae

page 20

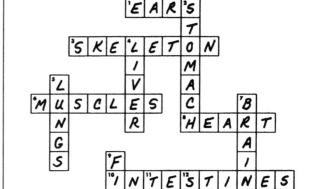

page 21

```
R F E C L A V I C H O M R D T S C
I P U M E T A P H L O A R A D I O
C O A X L S I S Y G F T I B O I A
O R O R B S U Z Y E I I B U I L X
S C R I I D I O L P R P Z Y G O
C S R Y D E H Y O C A L U P A C S
O L U A N H T A M I T E M M P T O
P A R L A Y A B V E A R I E T E
A S C L M L G I A T N O R F A
I R A E V Y T O A L L L N A M D X
T A P T Z D S I R C L U F E M U O
E T R A A I G D O H M R P H A L C
T A L P N O R F P H A L A N G E S
L T S S Z Y G O M A T I C Y H D O
L E O Y Y H U M E R U S U L T R A
A M A L U B I E T A L C V I C L E
```

Answers

page 25

Answers will vary. Possible answers include:
1. it controls the majority of the other bodily functions
2. they need to protect the organs inside of them
3. skeletal muscles are attached to bones and allow the bones to move in different directions
4. they are used every day to chew many different kinds of foods
5. the cells in the body need fresh blood to survive
6. these traits are inherited genetically; that is, this information is stored in the chromosomes given to you by your parents
7. the shape of the organ is essential to the function it performs
8. each part of our body sends messages to the brain, and the nerves carry back the brain's response

page 26

1. anvil
2. retina
3. dermis
4. pelvis
5. pancreas
6. hormones
7. tibia
8. femur
9. marrow
10. hypothermia
11. larynx
12. palate

page 28

Symmetrical body parts are: brain, rib cage, face, eyes, lungs, and teeth.

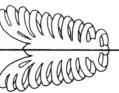

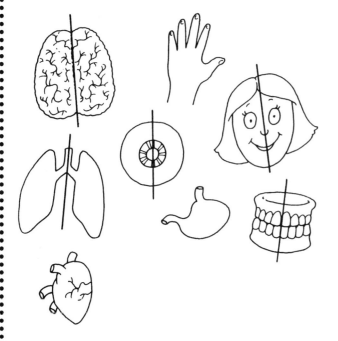

page 34

Answers will vary. Possible answers include:

1. Turn left out of the room. Make a right at Room 116. Turn right at the second corridor.
2. Make a left out of Room 128 and go down two doors. Turn left into the pharmacy.
3. Turn left out of Room 110. Go past the elevator and down two doors on the right to the general supplies room.
4. Turn right out of Room 116 and make a quick right. Go to the end of the corridor and make a left. Turn right into the recovery room.
5. Go straight out of the operating room to the end of the corridor. The medical supply closet is directly in front of you.

page 36

a. capillaries—2
b. plasma—6
c. veins—9
d. red blood cells—3
e. platelets—7
f. pulse—10
g. leukocyte—4
h. marrow—5
i. arteries—8
j. hemoglobin—1

page 42

1. 25 pounds
2. Sara; Craig and Julie
3. Benny
4. Benny and Missy
5. Max
6. 5' 1"
7. 1 1/2 pounds
8. Answers will vary.

page 52

1. e
2. j
3. g
4. b
5. a
6. h
7. c
8. f
9. d
10. i

Answers

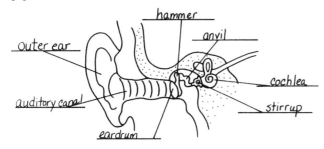

Answers for the second part of this exercise will vary. Possible answers include:

outer ear—allows sounds to enter the auditory canal and be processed by the middle ear and inner ear

hammer—one of the small bones in the middle ear that helps to process sound waves

anvil—one of the bones that connects the eardrum to the oval window in the inner ear

auditory canal—the place where sounds enter the ear. Sounds are processed through the auditory canal to the eardrum

eardrum—vibrates when sounds hit it. The vibrations are then picked up by the hammer, anvil, and stirrup and processed in the inner ear

stirrup—smallest bone in the body. The stirrup connects the middle ear and inner ear

cochlea—has three ducts, one of which has thousands of tiny hair cells that form the organ of Corti, which is the hearing organ

page 54

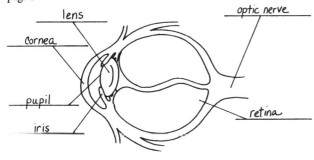

Answers for the second part of this exercise will vary. Possible answers include:

iris—contains *melanin*, a substance that gives the eye its color and absorbs brilliant light that could harm the eye

pupil—controls the amount of light coming into the eye

cornea—is in front of the iris and allows light to enter the eyeball

lens—a clear disk that constantly changes shape to make images sharp and focused

optic nerve—connects the eyeball to the brain

retina—changes light rays into electrical impulses that are sent to the brain; allows a person to have peripheral vision

page 55

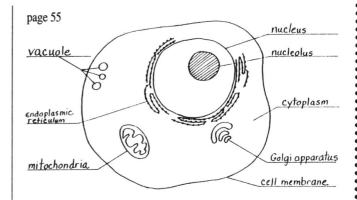

page 56

1. red blood cell
2. nerve cell
3. muscle cell
4. epidermal cell
5. fibroblast cell

Answers for the second part of this exercise will vary.

page 58

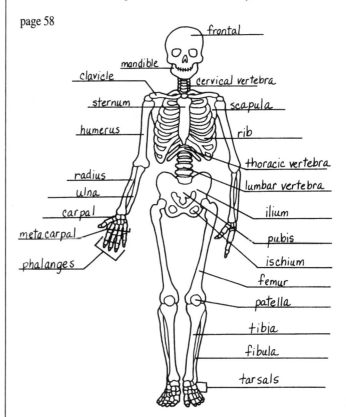

Answers

page 59
1. 100,000
2. 4
3. 32
4. 3
5. 206
6. 1,500
7. 26
8. 27
9. 2,000,000,000
10. 28

page 69
Breakfast calories
```
    935
    600
    840
  1,650
+   360
  -----
  4,385
```

Lunch calories
```
  4,160
    600
    720
+ 1,600
  -----
  7,080
```

Dinner calories
```
  1,530
  1,200
    675
    720
    600
      0
+ 2,450
  -----
  7,175
```
Zelda consumed 18,640 calories all day.

page 74
Answers will vary.